PEACE &
POSSIBILITIES

Creating Peace of Mind
in Retirement

Revised Edition

RHETT WOOD & MARK ROSE

authorHOUSE®

AuthorHouse™
1663 Liberty Drive
Bloomington, IN 47403
www.authorhouse.com
Phone: 1 (800) 839-8640

Published by AuthorHouse 02/27/2019

ISBN: 978-1-5462-3967-3 (sc)
ISBN: 978-1-5462-3969-7 (e)

Library of Congress Control Number: 2018905043

Print information available on the last page.

This book is printed on acid-free paper.

This book discusses general concepts for retirement planning and is not intended to provide tax or legal advice. Individuals are urged to consult with their tax and legal professionals regarding these issues. It is important to know: a) insurance and investment instruments and some of their features have costs associated with them; b) annuities used to fund IRAs do not afford any additional measure of tax deferral for the IRA owner; c) income received from insurance and investment instruments may be taxable; and d) securities' past performance does not influence or predict future results. All stories are hypothetical and not intended to infer any client testimonials.

Throughout this book we refer to our two companies - Retirement Income Strategies and Investment Strategies. Financial planning and investment advisory services are offered by Investment Strategies, LLC, a Registered Investment Advisor in the state of Oklahoma. Insurance products and services are offered through Retirement Income Strategies, LLC. Investment Strategies, LLC and Retirement Income Strategies, LLC are affiliated companies.

Acknowledgments

We would like to thank our families for their love, encouragement and patience. Above all, we wish to thank and honor our Lord and Savior, whom we serve.

We would like to dedicate this book to our families who taught us the value of hard work, perseverance, honesty, and so many more character traits. Most importantly, they taught us to love the Lord and keep Him above all other things. This foundation has allowed us to become who we are today - thank you. We are eternally grateful to you and love you so much.

RETIREMENT INCOME
— STRATEGIES —

INVESTMENT
STRATEGIES

We are an independent financial planning firm in south Oklahoma City. We focus on creating income plans and operate as fiduciaries that serve our clients for their best interest. We offer insurance investments through Retirement Income Strategies, LLC and stock market security investments through Investment Strategies, LLC. We have been named as one of the Top 5 Financial Planners from The Oklahoman Reader's Choice Awards for the last seven years. Both of our advisors have been on local news stations and contributed to national news stories. We record a weekly podcast called *The One About Retirement* on a variety of retirement planning and financial topics and regularly host educational seminars on retirement planning, social security benefits and investments. Visit our website at **RetirementIncomeOK.com.**

Contents

Introduction

When you are young and working your first job, you want to earn enough money to support yourself. When you get married and start a family, you want to earn enough to care for your family and provide for their future. When your children are grown and out of the house, you begin to turn your attention to retirement. Once you retire you will still be providing for yourself and pursuing a whole new set of dreams. The goal of this book is to help ensure you have financial peace of mind during the retirement phase of your life.

Financial peace of mind in retirement is not achieved by accumulating assets. Rather, it is achieved by establishing *sustainable income streams* that are sufficient to maintain your standard of living as long as you are alive.

The best way to ensure you have financial peace of mind during retirement is to start planning now. Focus, as soon as possible, on creating a strategic, thoughtful plan for your financial well-being and future. This singular act of planning will yield both financial peace of mind and a defined path to help you fulfill your dreams. The first and perhaps most crucial step in the planning process is selecting a financial professional to work with.

SELECTING AN ADVISOR

Most people seek financial advice from one of three types of financial professionals:

Insurance agents: These individuals represent one or more insurance companies, sell insurance products, and are paid commissions based on what they sell. Because insurance agents are not fiduciaries, they can place their own interest or their company's interest before the client's interest.

Registered representatives or "Brokers:" These professionals typically work as an intermediary between the buyer and the financial companies selling various products, such as stocks, bonds, mutual funds, etc. Like insurance agents, brokers are paid commissions when their clients buy financial instruments. Brokers are not fiduciaries and can also place their own interest before that of their client.

Registered Investment Advisor (RIA): RIAs are firms whose financial advisors provide recommendations, analysis and services to help individuals and businesses manage their investment portfolios. An advisor within an RIA who is charged with providing investment advice is technically referred to as an "Investment Advisor Representative". RIAs are required to register either with the Securities and Exchange Commission (SEC) or state securities authorities. As a result, they are subject to the supervision of those bodies. RIAs are compensated by fees based on the amounts of investments managed; therefore, RIAs have a clear incentive to grow their clients' portfolios. Most importantly, advisors that work within an RIA structure have a fiduciary duty to their clients.

FIDUCIARY VS. SUITABILITY

A fiduciary duty involves trust, especially regarding the relationship between an advisor and a client. RIAs are fiduciaries. Advisors that operate within RIAs are legally obligated to act solely in the best interest of their clients. Among other rules, RIAs are bound to a "duty of loyalty" that requires its advisors to avoid conflicts and place the clients' interest above the advisors' own. In other words, advisors who commit to acting in a fiduciary capacity are held to a strict standard: they must, in every case, provide advice and services that are in their clients' best interests.

Insurance agents and brokers are held only to a suitability standard, which means they must only provide advice and services that are suitable. It does not mean they must offer you the best product. It simply means they may sell you a product that could be considered a workable solution. If there happens to be a product that pays double the commission, but it's not the best product for your situation, an agent or broker who is only held to a suitability standard is within his or her rights to recommend it.

This "less than the best" standard is a well-hidden, rarely discussed reality in the financial world.

When you are planning your financial future and making decisions that impact you and your loved ones, you should choose an advisor who is obligated to a fiduciary standard and who must do what is best for you and your family.

INVESTMENT STRATEGIES, LLC

We strongly believe in being held to a fiduciary standard; so much so that since 2007 we have operated within a RIA firm that was named Bertrand Wealth Strategies. At the beginning of 2017, Rhett Wood purchased Bertrand Wealth Strategies and changed the name to Investment Strategies, LLC. Through Investment Strategies we provide planning services and investment vehicles, and do so with the clients' interests always placed first.

RETIREMENT INCOME STRATEGIES, LLC

Brad and Carrie Bertrand founded the company that is now Retirement Solutions in

1998. Mark and Rhett worked several years under Retirement Solutions. We have now rebranded and our new company is Retirement Income Strategies, LLC. It is through this company that all insurance related products and services are offered.

THE PLANNING PROCESS

We use a five-step approach to explore key areas that are fundamental to successful retirement planning. You will be confident knowing that you have given careful consideration to risk exposure, income planning and legacy planning. This process involves:

- **Step 1 – Selecting a Financial Services Professional**

  Step One explains the role of a financial services professional and introduces our planning process.

- **Step 2 – Fact and Feeling Finding**

  Step Two encompasses thought-provoking questions about your financial well-being. It begins with the Color of Money Risk

Analysis and incorporates the elements of discovery and client feedback.

- **Step 3 – Retirement Planning**
  Step Three allows us to craft a retirement plan based on your goals and objectives, which is presented using the Retirement Income Plan, Color of Money and Social Security Maximization Reports. This allows us to engage in the important task of feedback prior to execution.

- **Step 4 – Solutions and Execution**
  Step Four incorporates solutions based on careful consideration of your risk exposure, income planning and legacy planning.

- **Step 5 – Ongoing Relationship**
  Step Five addresses long-term client engagement and five-star service by providing you with unique technology and enhanced value-adds, such as, the Generational Vault and RFID Data Blocker Cards.

These five steps require ongoing communication between the client and the advisor, either on a scheduled or "as needed" basis, so that the plan can be adjusted as major life events occur. This planning process continues for life and should involve your spouse, if you have one, and may even involve other family members.

RETIREMENT INCOME PLAN

At Retirement Income Strategies and Investment Strategies, our mission is to provide each client with financial peace of mind. The most important step in achieving this mission is to create and update a comprehensive, customized retirement plan. We call this plan a Retirement Income Plan and it has two crucial components:

- Income component: this part of the plan projects a lifetime income strategy. It will help secure income for your lifetime, no matter how long you live or how the investment markets perform.

- Growth component: this part of the plan projects the growth of assets not needed for income. These assets may be used later for unanticipated expenses or unplanned purchases throughout retirement. They also may simply pass on to your beneficiaries at your death with minimal cost, delay or taxation.

THE TEAM

Rhett Wood was recruited to New York Life in 2011 where he worked for two years. During this time, he received both his insurance and security licenses. Rhett graduated with a Bachelor of Science from Southern Nazarene University. He believes that God led him to the financial services industry. Rhett has a passion for helping others reach their retirement goals, because of this he conducts numerous retirement planning programs and has been featured on many local television and radio stations. He serves his clients in a fiduciary capacity as an Investment Advisor Representative and also as a licensed Insurance Agent. He attends Woodland Hills Baptist Church in Newcastle, OK and is not married.

Mark Rose is a native of Ardmore, OK and earned both his bachelor's and master's degrees from The University of Oklahoma. Mark serves his clients in a fiduciary capacity as an Investment Advisor Representative who holds his Series 65 Securities License, specializing in Social Security maximization and retirement planning. Mark has a strong background in education and enjoys helping his clients learn about retirement planning. He has been married for 23 years, has two daughters and attends Emmaus Baptist Church in south Oklahoma City.

BIBLICAL FINANCIAL PRINCIPLES

Retirement Income Strategies and Investment Strategies follow biblical financial principles in their planning processes, with the goal of aligning every decision with God's wisdom to establish and protect the financial well-being of their clients. Biblical financial principles that are utilized in every plan include:

- **Avoid speculation. Focus on provision, not riches.**
  "Do not weary yourself to gain wealth, cease from your consideration of it. When you set your eyes on it, it is gone. For wealth certainly makes itself wings, like an eagle that flies toward the heavens." Proverbs 23:4-5 NASB

- **Live within your means. Operate within a budget.**

  "For which one of you, when he wants to build a tower, does not first sit down and calculate the cost, to see if he has enough to complete it." Luke 14:28 NASB

- **Give generously.**

  "One gives freely, yet grows all the richer; another withholds what he should give, and only suffers want. Whoever brings blessing will be enriched, and one who waters will himself be watered." Proverbs 4:24-25 NASB

- **Plan ahead.**

  "The plans of the diligent lead surely to abundance, but everyone who is hasty comes only to poverty." Proverbs 21:5 NASB

- **Understand that God owns it all.**

  "The earth is the Lord's, and all it contains, the world, and those who dwell in it." Psalm 24:1 NASB

If you feel Retirement Income Strategies and Investment Strategies can serve you and your family, we would be honored to offer our support and expertise. It is our goal to help our clients enjoy the financial peace of mind that comes from the complete retirement and growth planning process that we have developed. Please consider this book an introduction to that planning process and know that you are welcome to contact us to arrange a free consultation and receive a complimentary Retirement Income Plan. We look forward to helping you lead a bountiful life and leave a meaningful family legacy.

HOW MUCH WILL YOU NEED?

Luke 14:28 NIV

Suppose one of you wants to build a tower.
Won't you first sit down and estimate the cost to
see if you have enough money to complete it?

When potential clients come to us, we always want to get to know them before we discuss finances. If the prospective clients are a couple, we want to hear how they met, if they have children and grandchildren, what those children and grandchildren are like, what the couple dreams of doing in their days of retirement, and what possible challenges they see ahead. If the prospective client is single, we want to know about their past and what they want their future to look like. The questions we are asked from all of our prospective clients are, "Will I have enough to comfortably retire?" or "Can I maintain my present standard of living without running out of money?" We respond by outlining the first steps of our process. We need to:

- Determine what you are spending now and project what you will be spending in the future.
- Determine what sustainable income streams you already have and what sustainable income streams we can create to maintain your standard of living.

We can begin to answer those questions only when we have the information we need.

We use a standard process to figure out what you're spending now and project what you will be spending in the future. First, we determine your average monthly income and if you are adding to savings each month. If your saving's balance is consistently going up, your monthly expenses are less than your income. If your saving's balance is not increasing, you are probably spending all of your income. We use this analysis to determine the average monthly amount required to maintain your present lifestyle. For example, if your monthly take-home income is $6,000 and you spend $5,500 per month, then you are saving an average of $500 per month. We then factor in any large future purchases and new future expenses. Lastly, we must consider any present expenses you will not incur in the future. Once we have done all this we have an idea of how much you presently spend per month and can calculate approximately how much you will spend going forward.

Of course, the biggest unknown in retirement planning is longevity. While your grandparents might have planned for 15 to 20 years of retirement, you may have a much longer planning horizon. Many of today's soon-to-be retirees need to plan for 25 to 30 years of retirement. It's a good problem to have, and fear not, we can help you create a lasting plan. To determine how long we must plan for, we use life expectancy tables and then make adjustments based on your present health condition and family history.

In addition to longevity, there are three other key considerations that must be addressed when determining future expenses. They are inflation, taxes and long-term care costs.

Inflation. Inflation is essentially a decrease in the purchasing power of money. What a gallon of milk costs today might cost double or triple twenty years in the future, depending on the rate of inflation. A peace of mind retirement plan takes into account the effect of inflation so that you don't have to worry about the future cost of that gallon of milk or anything else.

One possible inflation scenario goes something like this: You're planning for retirement back in 1990, in that year you work with your Registered Investment Advisor and determine that your current expenses are $3,500 per month. When you retire in 2019, you will actually need almost $7,000 to buy the same amount of goods or services as you did in 1990.[1] As you catch your breath, you also spend a few moments being grateful that you consulted someone who considers inflation and plans for it as well.

It is irresponsible to create a retirement plan that doesn't account for inflation—our plans factor in inflation.

Taxes. During working years, taxable income generally increases, therefore taxes generally increase. In retirement, taxable income often levels off or decreases, causing taxes to remain steady or decline. We take a conservative approach and assume taxes will gradually increase unless there is a compelling reason to assume otherwise.

Long-term care costs. A study by Medicare reveals that a majority of people 65 and older will need long-term care services and support at some time during their lives.[2] If you haven't planned for those costs, they can be the undoing of even the most robust retirement plan. In Oklahoma during 2019, the annual cost for a semi-private nursing home room was $57,333. The annual cost for homemaker services, such as grocery shopping, errands, cleaning and cooking, was $47,133.[3]

It's easy to see how, without a plan, long-term care costs could quickly drain a lifetime of savings. Fortunately, there are options that allow you to plan for the costs of long-term care without siphoning off the money you need to maintain your lifestyle. These options are used in the plans we design for our clients and are more fully discussed in Chapter Ten.

In retirement, many retirees have to choose which bills to pay or which prescriptions to fill because they don't have enough income to pay for all of their necessary expenses. That is not a "peace of mind" retirement. It is critical that we accurately project the average amount you will spend each month for the rest of your life so we know how much income you will need in the future.

CHAPTER 1 RECAP

- Because spending patterns are set well before you retire, and are generally maintained throughout your lifetime, your current expenses can be used to project future expenses. Your spending levels can be adjusted, but realistic retirement plans begin with projected future expenses moderately above what you presently spend and increase over time.

- Chances are you will have a much longer life than your grandparents or even parents. Unless there are extenuating circumstances, it is crucial you plan for at least 25 to 30 years of retirement income.

- Be sure to take into account the powerful issues of inflation, taxes and long-term care costs when planning for how much income you need to retire. These costs can dramatically affect your savings and comfort in retirement. Many plans underestimate or fail altogether to recognize these costs.

[1] - *Bureau of Labor Statistics Inflation Calculator. https://www.bls.gov/data/inflation_calculator.htm*

[2] - *https://Longtermcare.acl.gov/the-basics/index.html*

[3] - *https://www.genworth.com/about-us/industry-expertise/cost-of-care.html*

RETIREMENT INCOME PLAN

Proverbs 21:5 NASB
*The plans of the diligent lead surely to abundance,
but everyone who is hasty comes only to poverty.*

In 2014, the International Foundation of Employee Benefit Plans conducted an online retirement survey for National Employee Benefits Day. The greatest retirement benefit according to the survey was getting to wake up without an alarm clock. The greatest retirement fear was not having enough money to live comfortably for the rest of their lives. Fortunately, this fear can be mitigated by ongoing planning.

At Retirement Income Strategies and Investment Strategies we construct and update a plan that ensures each client will have more than enough income to maintain his or her standard of living—no matter how long he or she lives! This plan is called the Retirement Income Plan and is why our clients can enjoy financial peace of mind either before retirement or in retirement. Like we said in the Introduction, each plan has two crucial components - Income and Growth.

The Income component projects your lifetime income streams, ensuring you don't outlive your income no matter how long you live or how the investment markets perform.

The Growth component projects the growth of assets not needed for income. These assets may be used later for unanticipated expenses or unplanned purchases throughout retirement. They will likely pass on to your beneficiaries at your death, with minimal cost, delay and taxation.

INCOME GAP

Once you start drawing Social Security, it will provide a reliable source of income for the rest of your life. These benefits alone will likely be insufficient to fund the lifestyle you desire. You may also have other dependable income sources, such as pensions, rental income, mineral rights income, investment income, etc. Your income sources combined may or may not be sufficient to provide the retirement lifestyle you desire. Your personalized Retirement Income Plan will project both the expenses you will incur during your lifetime and the amount of income you can expect to generate during your lifetime. If your plan projects that your expenses exceed your income sources, you will have an income gap. To fill this income gap we can utilize financial assets you already own to create additional lifetime income sources. There are specific investments that are designed to generate lifetime income.

If you are like many Americans, you may have funds in market-driven investments that were acquired over time. You cannot assess with certainty the income these assets will provide toward your retirement because their value is market-driven. If the market goes down while you are drawing from these accounts you could exhaust the accounts. To address this uncertainty we can redeploy some portion of your market-driven investments into fixed-indexed annuities that can generate stable, lifelong retirement income streams much like Social Security or pension benefits.

To determine if a fixed-indexed annuity fits your situation, start by asking yourself the following questions:

- Are you concerned about finding secure financial vehicles to protect your retirement savings and generate future income?
- Are you concerned that investments in the market may lose value or be insufficient to meet your future income needs?

If you answered yes to either of these questions, you might consider a fixed-indexed annuity. Some of the advantages and disadvantages of fixed-indexed annuities are discussed below and later in Chapter Seven.

HOW ANNUITIES FIT INTO A RETIREMENT PLAN

Fixed-indexed annuities are popular, flexible and reliable investments that allow you to generate lifetime income. One of the main advantages of a fixed-indexed annuity with lifetime income is that once the income is started, it will pay you a monthly check for the remainder of your life. If you have an income gap, your customized

Retirement Income Plan will show when and how much income you will need to fill it. Equipped with this vital information, we can recommend the best fixed-indexed annuity to meet your specific income need. We will also make sure you understand the features, benefits and costs of any annuity we recommend.

A fixed-indexed annuity with an income rider is often used to fill a client's income gap. The income rider allows you to know the minimum income your annuity will pay you for life, starting at a specific time in the future. The income rider creates a separate account, called the income account. This income account value is a calculated number and is only used to determine the amount of income the annuity pays you. An income account is typically larger than the annuity's cash value, and it will increase over time, often at a fixed rate. The income the annuity generates is based on your age when you begin taking income and the amount in the income account. The annuity payment lasts for life - even if the annuity cash value is eventually exhausted. The income guarantee is based on the claims-paying ability of the insurance company issuing the annuity, which is why it is important to select a well-rated company.

The main disadvantage of fixed-indexed annuities is that they are long-term investments subject to surrender charges. In the state of Oklahoma, fixed-indexed annuities can have a surrender period of up to ten years with a decreasing surrender charge starting as high as thirteen percent. Some states allow longer surrender periods and larger surrender penalties. Most fixed-indexed annuities do allow penalty-free annual withdraws of up to ten percent of the accumulation value of the annuity after the first year, but withdrawal percentages may vary.

Another type of annuity that can be used to fill the income gap is a Single Premium Immediate Annuity (SPIA). A SPIA is simply a contract between the annuity owner and an insurance company. SPIAs are structured so that the owner pays a lump sum of money (a single premium) to an insurance company, and the insurance company gives the owner a guaranteed income over an agreed upon time period or over their lifetime. Again, any guarantee from an insurance company is based on the claims-paying ability of the issuing insurance company. It is, therefore, important to select a well-rated company.

While there is general faith that the market will trend up over the long-term, you may not wish to take the risk of losing money in a fluctuating market. Beyond market volatility, interest rates also come with an inherent level of uncertainty, making it hard to create a dependable future income stream on your own. SPIAs reduce these risks by giving you regular income payments that can begin the moment you buy the contract.

However, Single Premium Immediate Annuities (SPIAs) are a less popular means of filling an income gap compared to fixed-indexed annuities with income riders because once the SPIA payment stream begins it cannot be changed. Because of this lack of flexibility, we rarely recommend SPIAs. We discuss annuities in more depth in Chapter Seven.

OTHER SOURCES OF LIFETIME INCOME

Social Security. Social Security is the most common source of lifetime retirement income. Unfortunately, many people do not receive their maximum lifetime Social Security benefits because they begin taking their Social Security benefits at the less-than-optimal time, or they fail to use the most beneficial filing strategy for their situation. The next chapter discusses how to choose the optimal time and manner to receive your Social Security benefit so you and your spouse, if you have a spouse, will receive your maximum lifetime Social Security benefits.

Pensions. Pensions were once the most reliable source of retirement income, but they have become increasingly scarce in recent decades. That said, pensions do still exist, and in fact, some people have several of them, resulting from working several jobs that offer pensions. Pensions are defined benefit plans, structured and managed by your employer. They typically require (or allow) no management from the employee.

You might be owed pension payments from a previous job and not even realize it. If you think you might be eligible for a pension, or you aren't sure, it's worth checking. According to the Pension Benefit Guarantee Corporation, more than 38,000 Americans haven't claimed pension benefits they are owed, resulting in more than $300 million dollars of unclaimed benefits.[1]

Mineral rights. Mineral rights that can be leased or that can provide royalties have the potential to be an income source for life. However, income from mineral rights is less reliable than Social Security or a pension income and is therefore used in most retirement plans as a temporary source of income.

Mineral rights can also be sold outright and the proceeds reinvested in more reliable income producing assets. Deciding what to do with your mineral rights and how to structure them to optimize your income are decisions we can help you with.

Inheritance. Baby Boomers are expected to receive $8.4 trillion in inheritances.[2] Unfortunately, only 15 percent of all Boomers will actually participate in this wealth transfer and less than 10 percent of those will receive at least a six figure inheritance.[3] But, if you are one of those lucky people receiving a significant inheritance and you handle this inheritance wisely it can make a huge difference in the security and comfort of your retirement. On the other hand, if you make any number of common inheritance mistakes you can end up with a huge tax bill you must pay. Even worse, those sudden, large amounts of money seem to disappear much more quickly than carefully distributed, monthly payouts.

We can help you and your loved ones receive maximum benefit from inheritances.

CHAPTER 2 RECAP

- We create a personalized Retirement Income Plan for each client. The retirement income portion of the plan projects both lifetime income needs and lifetime income sources. If income needs exceed income sources then there is an "income gap" that must be filled.

- To fill an "income gap", one of the financial instruments we recommend using is a fixed-indexed annuity with an income rider. This instrument will generate monthly income for life at any chosen time in the future.

- The growth portion of the Retirement Income Plan projects the value of the assets that are not used for income generation. These assets can be used to supplement projected income or can be passed on to heirs. Legacy assets are discussed in detail in Chapter Four.

- Other common lifetime income sources include Social Security, pensions, mineral rights, and an inheritance. These income sources each have their own benefits and risks that must be considered when you rely upon them for your retirement. Social Security will be discussed more fully in Chapter Three.

[1] - *http://www.pbgc.gov/about/who-we-are/retirement-matters/post/2013/01/14/Does-PBGC-Owe-You-Almost-$1-Million.aspx*

[2] - *http://www.forbes.com/2011/02/15/baby-boomers-retirement-how-to-make-the-most-of-your-inheritance.html*

[3]   -   *http://www.investopedia.com/articles/retirement/12/inheritancebust.asp*

OPTIMIZING YOUR SOCIAL SECURITY BENEFITS

Proverbs 13:16 TLB
A wise man thinks ahead;
a fool doesn't, and even brags about it.

Two of my (Mark) clients were contemplating when to retire and when was the best time to start their Social Security benefits. They originally planned to wait to begin receiving their Social Security benefits until they each turned 70 years old, the age when their monthly checks would be at their maximum amounts. Until then they would work part-time and would take income from other investments necessary to meet their monthly needs. They thought that waiting until age 70 to begin receiving their monthly benefit checks would be the best choice long-term. As they later discovered, the best choice often requires using one or more special options that most people do not know about.

When they came in to talk with me about their choices, I ran a Social Security Maximization report for them. After entering all the necessary information from their Social Security statements, we reviewed their report and they were surprised by the results. They expected the Maximization Report to simply confirm their decision to wait until age 70 to begin receiving their Social Security benefits. Instead, the report suggested, in detail, an entirely different approach to taking their Social Security benefits that would generate much greater combined lifetime benefit amounts.

Social Security is the bedrock of most retirement plans in America. Choosing the best time to begin receiving your Social Security benefits may seem easy, but it is not. Most people make this critical decision without considering or utilizing one of several special Social Security benefit options. In fact, choosing when and how to take your Social Security benefit is one of the most complex and important decisions you will make in retirement.

SOCIAL SECURITY BASICS

Here are some facts that illustrate how Americans currently use Social Security:

- 90 percent of Americans age 65 and older receive Social Security benefits.[1]
- Social Security provides about 33 percent of the income of the elderly.[1]
- Claiming Social Security benefits at the wrong time for you or your spouse can reduce your monthly benefit by up to 65 percent.[2]

- In 2013, more than half of workers claimed Social Security benefits as soon they became eligible.[3]
- In 2019, the average monthly Social Security benefit for retired workers is $1,462. The maximum benefit at Full Retirement Age for 2019 is $2,861.[4]

Let's start by covering the basic information about Social Security which should give you an idea of where you stand. Just as the foundation of a house creates a stable platform for the rest of the framework to rest upon, your Social Security benefit is the foundation of your retirement plan. The purpose of the information is not to give an exhaustive explanation of how Social Security works, but to give you some tools and questions to start understanding how Social Security affects your retirement and how you can prepare for it.

Eligibility. Understanding how and when you are eligible for Social Security benefits will help clarify what to expect when the time comes to claim them.

In most cases, Americans born after 1929 must earn 40 quarters of credit to be eligible to draw their Social Security retirement benefit. In 2019, a Social Security credit represents $1,360 earned in a calendar quarter. The number changes as it is indexed each year. In 2018, a credit represented $1,320. Four quarters of credit is the maximum number that can be earned each year. In 2019, an American would have had to earn at least $5,440 to accumulate four credits.

To receive Spousal Benefits, you must be at least 62 years old and have been married to a recipient of Social Security benefits for at least 12 months. The longer one waits past the age of 62 to receive spousal benefits, the greater the benefit becomes.

It is important to know that once you claim your Social Security benefit, you have one year to change your mind. If you do change your mind you must repay, with interest, all benefits paid within that first year. Once you have been receiving benefits for a year, you are locked into that base benefit amount forever. There may be a cost of living adjustments added to your base over time, however. In 2019, the Cost of Living Adjustment (COLA) was 2.8%.

Primary Insurance Amount. Your Primary Insurance Amount (PIA) is the amount of your Social Security benefit at your Full Retirement Age (FRA). You can think of your PIA as a ripening fruit. Your Social Security benefit becomes ripe at your FRA. If you opt to take benefits before your FRA, your monthly benefit will be less than your PIA. You will essentially be picking an unripened fruit. If you wait until after your FRA to access your benefits, then your benefits will exceed your PIA. You don't want to wait too long to access your benefits because every month you wait is one less check you get from the government—there is an optimal time to begin receiving your benefits. In other words, the fruit gets sweeter as it ripens but you don't want to let it over-ripen.

Full Retirement Age. Your FRA is an important figure for anyone who is planning to rely on Social Security benefits in their retirement. Depending on when you were born, there is a specific age at which you will attain FRA. Your FRA is dictated by your year of birth, and is the age at which you can begin your full monthly benefit. Your FRA is important because it is half of the equation used to calculate your Social Security benefit. The other half of the equation is based on when you start taking benefits.

When Social Security was initially set up, the FRA was age 65, and it still is for people born before 1938. But as time has passed, the age for receiving full retirement benefits has increased. If you were born between 1938 and 1960, your full retirement age is somewhere on a sliding scale between 65 and 67. Anyone born in 1960 or later will now have to wait until age 67 for full benefits. Increasing the FRA has helped the government reduce the cost of the Social Security program, which pays out almost $1 trillion dollars to beneficiaries every year![5]

Year of Birth	Full Retirement Age
1943-1954	66
1955	66 and 2 months
1956	66 and 4 months
1957	66 and 6 months
1958	66 and 8 months
1959	66 and 10 months
1960 or later	67[6]

While you can begin collecting benefits as early as age 62, the amount you receive as a monthly benefit will be less than it would be if you wait until you reach or surpass your FRA.

It is important to note that if you file for Social Security benefits before your FRA, ***the reduction to your monthly benefit will remain in place for the rest of your life.*** At FRA, 100 percent of your PIA is available as a monthly benefit. You can also delay receiving benefits up to age 70, in which case your benefits will be higher than your PIA for the rest of your life. At age 70, your monthly benefit reaches its maximum and will no longer increase.

ROLLING UP YOUR SOCIAL SECURITY

Your Social Security income "rolls up" the longer you wait to claim it. This means that every year you wait to start your benefit, the monthly amount you will receive increases. Your monthly benefit will continue to increase until you turn 70 years old.

OPTING TO RECEIVE SOCIAL SECURITY BENEFITS EARLY

For many people, receiving their Social Security benefits as soon as possible seems best and indeed may be best. For example, many people need to rely on Social Security on day one of their retirement. In fact, 51 percent of 62-year-old Americans file for Social Security benefits. However, many of those taking an early benefit at age 62 are simply under-informed about Social Security and are making this major decision based on rumors, misinformation and emotion. ***The difference between the best and worst Social Security decision can be tens of thousands of dollars over a lifetime of benefits.***

Appropriate reasons to file early for your benefit:

- You find your job unbearable so you retire early and you need income.
- You are not healthy and believe you will not live to your life expectancy.
- You are the surviving spouse and you have to start your benefits to make ends meet.

Appropriate reasons to delay taking your benefit:

- You want to maximize your retirement income.
- You want to increase retirement benefits for your spouse.
- You are still working and like it.
- You are healthy.

Remember, the longer you wait, the higher your monthly benefit amount becomes. But each month you wait is one less month that you receive a Social Security check. ***The primary goal is to maximize your lifetime benefits.***

SOCIAL SECURITY EARNINGS LIMIT

Another thing to consider before starting your Social Security benefit at age 62 is the Earnings Limit. The Social Security Earnings Limit is the amount of money you can earn before your earnings impact your Social Security benefit. If your income exceeds the Social Security income limit (which is defined based on your specific situation), your Social Security benefits will be reduced. If you are between ages 62 and the year before you turn Full Retirement Age and still working, in 2019 you may earn up to $17,640 before the Social Security Administration will deduct $1 from your benefit for every $2 you earn. In the year you turn your Full Retirement Age, the Earnings Limit will be $46,920 before the administration deducts $1 for every $3 you earn until the month you reach full retirement age.

It's important to note that the Earnings Limit does not apply if you file for benefits at your Full Retirement Age or beyond. These limits only apply to those who begin taking Social Security benefits before reaching Full Retirement Age.

Despite the importance of knowing when and how to take your Social Security benefit, many of today's retirees and pre-retirees know little about how to maximize their benefits. So, to whom should you turn for advice when making this complex decision? Before you pick up the phone and call Uncle Sam, you should know that the Social Security Administration (SSA) representatives are actually prohibited from giving you election advice. Plus, SSA representatives in general are trained to focus on monthly benefit amounts, not the maximum lifetime benefit.

MAXIMIZING YOUR LIFETIME BENEFIT

The three most common ages that people associate with retirement benefits are 62 (earliest eligible age under normal circumstances), Full Retirement Age (usually between ages 65 and 67), and 70 (age at which monthly maximum benefit is reached). In almost all circumstances, however, none of those three most common ages will give you the maximum lifetime benefit. As evidenced by the opening story of this chapter, calculating how to maximize **lifetime benefits** is far more complex than conducting a break-even analysis or simply waiting until age 70 for your maximum monthly benefit amount.

The Social Security options that can be used to maximize lifetime benefits don't stop with selecting the age to trigger your benefits. There are several types of Social Security benefits you must choose to use or not use in order to maximize your lifetime benefits.

Types of Social Security Benefits:

- *Retired Worker Benefit.* This is the benefit with which most people are familiar. The Retired Worker Benefit is what most people are talking about when they refer to Social Security. It is your benefit based on your earnings and the amount that you have paid into the system over the span of your career.

- *Spousal Benefit.* The Spousal Benefit is available to the spouse of someone who is eligible for Retired Worker Benefits.
- *Survivorship Benefit.* When one spouse passes away, the survivor is able to receive the larger of the two benefit amounts.

Social Security maximization is about getting the most Social Security income possible during your lifetime Our Social Security maximization software can identify both the year and month that it is most beneficial for you to file and the best Social Security benefit types to use when filing.

THE DIVORCE FACTOR

Divorce is devastating, and not just emotionally. The average cost of divorce is somewhere between $15,000 and $20,000, a price tag that comes nowhere close to the total financial damage that a divorce can have on families. It's shockingly easy to create divisions among even the closest of couples, **so one of the most important things to do—for your family and your family's finances and legacy—is to work on your marriage every day just like you work at your job.** Create a plan for maintaining your marriage and your family, just as you would create a plan for your retirement. It's the best investment you will ever make. With that said, how does a divorced spouse qualify for benefits? If you have gone through a divorce, it might affect the retirement benefit to which you are entitled. In general, a person can receive benefits as a divorced spouse on a former spouse's Social Security record so long as the following conditions are met:

- The marriage lasted at least 10 years; and
- The person filing for divorced benefits is at least age 62, unmarried, and not entitled to a higher Social Security benefit on his or her own record.[7]

Important Questions and Answers about Your Social Security Benefits:

- How can I maximize my lifetime benefits? You can maximize your lifetime Social Security benefits by knowing: 1) the optimal age to file; 2) which benefit types to use; and 3) when to use the benefit types. Retirement Income Strategies and Investment Strategies has the experience and the tools to help you maximize your lifetime benefits.

- Will the Social Security Administration provide me with the advice necessary to maximize my lifetime benefits? The Social Security Administration cannot provide you with advice necessary to maximize your lifetime benefits. They can give you information about your monthly benefit, but that's it. They can accurately answer how the system works, but they won't advise you on maximizing your lifetime benefits.

With all of the options of when to begin receiving Social Security and all of the options of which benefit strategies to use, you can see why filing for Social Security is extremely complex. This is especially true if you have a spouse and wish to maximize the lifetime benefits for each of you. Gathering data and learning about all the different benefit options, is not nearly enough to know what you must do to maximize your lifetime Social Security benefits. You can attempt to figure it all out and you might get it right, but you'll always wonder if you made the best decision. We can help you gain the peace of mind of knowing with certainty that you made the best decision.

The Social Security Maximization Report that Retirement Income Strategies will generate for you represents an invaluable resource for understanding how and when to file for your Social Security benefits. When you get your customized Social Security Maximization Report, you will not only know all the best options available to you—but you will understand the financial implications of each option. Most importantly, the report highlights *exactly* at what age—including which month—you should trigger benefits and how you should apply. The report will do the same for your spouse. The report also includes a variety of other time-specific recommendations, such as when to apply for Medicare or when to take Required Minimum Distributions from your qualified plans. The Social Security Maximization Report leaves no guesswork. It clearly explains what to do and when.

Once you know the best options available to you and your spouse, if you have a spouse, you can evaluate which option works best given your particular goals. Once you decide when and how you are going to receive your Social Security benefits, the specific income streams that will be created by your decision will be incorporated into your personalized Retirement Income Plan.

CHAPTER 3 RECAP

- The most common ages (under normal circumstances) that people choose to receive their Social Security benefits are 62 (earliest eligible age), 65 to 67 (Full Retirement Age), and 70 (age at which maximum monthly benefit is reached). In almost all circumstances, however, none of these ages will give you your maximum lifetime benefit.

- There are several different types of Social Security benefits. Filing for the right benefit type at the right time will help you maximize your lifetime Social Security benefit.

- In general, a person can receive benefits as a divorced spouse on a former spouse's Social Security record if he or she was married to the former spouse for at least 10 years; is at least 62 years old; is unmarried; and is not entitled to a higher Social Security benefit on his or her own record.

- If you have a spouse, identifying the best time to file for each of you in order to maximize your combined lifetime Social Security benefits is a very complex calculation. There are thousands of combinations of when to begin receiving benefits and what type of benefits to elect.

- While you can and should educate yourself about how Social Security works, the reality is you don't need to know a great deal about Social Security to make the best decision about when and how you should opt to receive your benefits. By inputting specific personal information in a software program we can generate a customized Social Security report that will tell you exactly how to maximize your lifetime benefits.

- A Social Security Maximization Report can identify the exact month you and your spouse, if you have one, should trigger your Social Security benefits and the types of benefits each of you should use and when.

- Once you determine when and how you are going to receive your Social Security benefits, the information is incorporated into your personalized Retirement Income Plan.

[1] - *https://www.ssa.gov/news/press/factsheets/basicfact-alt.pdf*

[2] - *https://www.ssa.gov/planners/retire/retirechart.html*

[3] - *Trends in Social Security Claiming, Alicia H Munnell and Anqi Chen, Center for Retirement Research, May 2015. http://crr.bc.edu/wp-content/uploads/2015/05/IB_15-8.pdf*

[4] - *https://www.ssa.gov/policy/docs/quickfacts/stat_snapshot/index.html*

[5] - *http://www.ssa.gov/news/press/factsheets/basicfact-alt.pdf*

[6] - *http://www.ssa.gov/OACT/progdata/nra.html*

[7] - *http://www.ssa.gov/planners/retire/divspouse.html*

LEGACY ASSETS

Psalm 25:13 NASB

His soul shall abide in prosperity, and his descendants will inherit the land.

Once sufficient income streams are established to ensure you can maintain a comfortable retirement, your remaining financial assets should be conservatively invested to provide an additional safety net for unanticipated future expenses or purchases. We call these remaining assets Legacy Assets. Once you pass on, your Legacy Assets will create an inheritance for those you love and/ or for those causes you care about. Legacy Assets typically include bank and investment accounts, life insurance, personal and business property, your primary residence, vacation homes, time shares, etc.

Legacy Assets provide an important buffer to protect you from some of the major variables in retirement planning, including inflation, taxes, rising healthcare expenses, and the premature death of a spouse. During your lifetime, the legacy portion of your plan is always available to draw on in the event any of these variables adversely impacts your retirement plan. If the income side of your Retirement Income Plan sufficiently provides for all of your income needs, as it is designed to do, then the legacy side of your plan will eventually pass to your heirs, charities, church, mission organizations, etc.

In addition to providing back-up insurance for your retirement income, Legacy Assets could also be used to fund unanticipated purchases. Unanticipated purchases could include buying an RV to visit all of America's national parks, paying for a trip to Disney World with all of your grandkids, or acquiring a small cabin on a quiet lake. It is these types of purchases or expenditures you may be spending your kids' inheritance on, as the famous bumper sticker alludes. But more often than not, Legacy Assets and all of the growth from these assets will transfer to your heirs and favorite charities when you pass on.

Finally, the legacy side of your Retirement Income Plan is also available to draw on if you simply decide to increase your standard of living. Surprisingly, this is something that rarely happens. Once a standard of living is established it seldom changes, even when there is an unanticipated substantial sum of money introduced into an estate. It is nice to know you can upgrade your standard of living if you wish, however. When we talk about Legacy Assets, we are talking about both financial assets, such as investment accounts, and real assets, such as your primary residence, vacation homes or raw land. Because financial Legacy Assets are not expected to be used for lifetime income, they can and should be conservatively invested for growth. As mentioned above, if necessary, both financial and real Legacy Assets can be used to create more income or to pay for unanticipated purchases and expenses.

HOW INVESTING HAS CHANGED

When it comes to growing your financial Legacy Assets, you will have a number of investment options to choose from. These options will provide the full spectrum of risk and return. Based on your risk tolerance, you can decide what investments are appropriate. Before we discuss these investment options, let's look at some of the ways investing has changed over the years.

Advice about what to do with money has been around as long as money has existed. Hindsight allows us to see which advice was good and which advice was poor. Some sources of advice and some investment concepts that your parents used won't work today. Today, the best investment strategies are able to adapt to fluctuating economic conditions and changes in your life.

In the 1990s, interest rates were high and market volatility was low. At that time, you could invest in either equities or bonds and you were likely to be successful. To get an acceptable return you could choose either a market-driven investment with minimal risk or you could choose a fixed rate investment with little risk. Today, those same conditions do not exist. Market-driven investments have much higher volatility (risk) and interest rates on fixed rate investments are at all-time lows. Today it is more difficult to get an acceptable return without taking on some risk.

The market downturn of 2008-2009 demonstrated that the pursuit of acceptable returns was incredibly destructive to the retirement plans of millions of Americans. Depending on the market indicators used, investors lost between 30 to 50 percent of their portfolio values. Perhaps the most important lesson investors learned from the 2008-2009 downturn was that brokers and brokerage firms either did not understand the risks associated with the investments they recommended and sold, or they chose to ignore those risks. The last two weeks of 2018 saw the worst consecutive five-day market performance since that 2008 downturn. Failing to understand and account for these risks could destroy the retirement and legacy plans of millions and force millions more to postpone their retirement date.

INVESTING FINANCIAL LEGACY ASSETS

Managing your financial Legacy Assets is an ongoing process that deserves customization and requires adaptation to a changing world. Investments such as bank CDs, which worked for your parents and grandparents, can't even keep up with inflation today. Investments such as domestic Blue Chip stocks, commonly held by retirees of earlier generations, come with significant risk today. People in retirement or approaching retirement today need more than what CDs or Blue Chip stocks can offer.

Financial Legacy Assets are assets projected to be passed on to heirs but can be used at any point in the future, if needed. These are not assets projected to be used for income. As a result, these assets may be allocated to investments that have no minimum guarantee, are subject to loss, and have the potential to provide superior returns compared to investments structured to provide income. **It is best if the money you have invested in the market is money you are not relying on for income.**

The longer your investment timeframe, the better. Longer investment timeframes will smooth out the ups and downs of market volatility. Investment Strategies can recommend conservative, long-term investment options that have the potential to create rewarding returns.

Some traditional investments, such as mutual funds, commonly have high fees and expenses and lack transparency, making them less than ideal investment options for your financial Legacy Assets. It is imperative all investments be objectively evaluated so wise decisions can be made. In the next chapter, we will discuss two options we commonly recommend for growing your financial Legacy Assets.

EVALUATING INVESTMENTS

Below are a few factors you should consider when evaluating any investment you presently own or any investment you may purchase in the future.

The spin. The financial industry has made an extraordinary effort to make fees and expenses associated with financial tools unclear. Some investment vehicles, like mutual funds, are notoriously vague in terms of the fees you are paying. For example, you might be told about a mutual fund's annual two percent fee, but are you aware that you also might pay a fee every time the fund's manager makes a trade? What's more, many funds are excessively traded, and those funds also tend to have lower performance than others.[1] Trading isn't the only way a financial vehicle can rack up costs. If you are told that a particular product has no fees, consider these things: How do they advertise? How do they pay for the mailings that go out to investors? Who pays the salary of the product's manager? You can bet that all of those expenses are structured into what you will pay for the product. This is why having an advisor with a fiduciary duty (requiring him or her to make recommendations that are in your best interest only) is a huge asset when choosing a financial product for growth.

The facts. Whatever investment products you might consider, always get the facts from an unbiased report. If you already have an investment portfolio, it is a good idea to have an unbiased report run on that portfolio as well. What sort of report? There are a number of options, but one excellent investment report is Morningstar.

Morningstar Reports will show the actual fees and expenses for every mutual fund and variable annuity, allowing you to compare the spin with the facts and make the choice that's best for you and your family. These reports also provide a convenient rating system that ranks the investment from a one to five stars. Four and five-star rated investments are potential keepers.

Anything three stars or less doesn't belong in your portfolio.

Performance. When evaluating potential growth products, you will have to make a choice: do you want to maximize growth or minimize risk? In most cases, if you desire attractive growth, you will have to take on risk. That's just the way financial markets work. However, you might be able to get a similar investment that is performing better than the one you have, with the same or even less risk. Do you know how to make that comparison? One of the easiest ways is to have Investment Strategies analyze your present investment portfolio and produce a comparison chart showing how your present investment portfolio performs against alternative investment portfolios with the same or less risk. This report is free of charge.

CHAPTER 4 RECAP

- Once sufficient income sources are in place to meet your lifetime income needs, your Retirement Income Plan will project the growth of the assets not needed for income. These Legacy Assets can be used for future unexpected needs and desires, or will pass to your heirs and beneficiaries.

- Financial Legacy Assets are an important element of a retirement plan, especially in the early stages of planning when you have a longer investment timeframe and can afford to take more risk.

- Yesterday's investment strategies may not work today. We are in an extended economic cycle where interest rates have been at historic lows and are beginning to rise. Relative to inflation, traditional retirement investments such as CDs and US Treasury instruments are actually earning a negative rate of return. The next chapter explores attractive investment options for Legacy Assets that were not available to your parents.

- Investment Strategies can help you evaluate your current investment portfolio using Morningstar Reports and Portfolio Analysis Reports. Even if you are satisfied with your present investment portfolio, it's important to know what fees you are paying and how your portfolio is performing compared to other portfolios with similar or less risk.

---

[1] - *http://www.forbes.com/sites/mitchelltuchman/2014/02/19/a- hidden-way-mutual-funds-cost-you-money/*

STOCK MARKET AND PROFESSIONALLY MANAGED INVESTMENTS

Ecclesiastes 11:2 NIV

Invest in seven ventures, yes, in eight; you do not know what disaster may come upon the land.

Here is a hypothetical example of how Investment Strategies could help a future retiree:

> Janet is 65 years old and wants to retire in two years. She has a 401(k) account that she has contributed to for 26 years. She has some stocks that her late husband managed. Altogether, the stocks have a value of approximately $100,000 and

Janet is unsure of whether she should hold or sell the stocks. Janet also has $55,000 in a mutual fund that her sister recommended to her five years ago, and $30,000 in another mutual fund that she heard about at work. Both accounts are IRAs but she is unsure whether her IRAs are Roth or Traditional IRAs and when it is best to draw income from them. Janet is wondering what would happen to all these investments if something happens to her. But above all, Janet wants to know how much retirement income her financial assets will generate and will they be enough.

After learning about Janet's retirement goals and dreams, reviewing her investment portfolio, and gathering her specific Social Security information, we will first conduct a portfolio analysis and run a Social Security Maximization Report. Equipped with this information we will prepare a customized Retirement Income Plan. This plan will ensure

Janet generates sufficient income to maintain her standard of living, regardless of how long she lives or how the investment markets perform. This plan will also recommend where to conservatively invest the assets not needed to generate income. Finally, with the assistance of an attorney, we will coordinate Janet's Retirement Income Plan with an estate plan. After Janet passes on, this estate plan will allow all of her assets to be distributed in the most expedient, private, tax-efficient manner possible.

It is likely that you have invested in the stock market at some point in your life. Based on the long-run performance of the stock market, investing a portion of your portfolio in the market can be wise. Understanding the markets long-term performance will help you be comfortable with the market's volatility and help you establish appropriate long-term performance expectations. So let's examine the stock market's performance characteristics and discuss the difference between stock market index returns and individual portfolio returns.

Perhaps the best chart showing how the stock market performs over the long-term is shown on the next page. The S&P 500 is a market index that is comprised of the stock values of 500 companies listed on the New York Stock Exchange. The S&P 500 is the average performance of these 500 stocks and serves as a proxy for the performance of the stock market as a whole. There are other stock market indexes, such as the Dow Jones Industrial Average and the Russell 5000, to name just a few, but the S&P 500 is perhaps the most regarded index in the investment community.

From 1926 to 2018 the S&P 500 had positive annual performance 73% of the time, the average loss for down years was 14% and the average gain for up years was 22%. It is safe to say that the stock market makes money about three out of every four years and that the average gain per year is about 1/3 higher than average loss per year.

THE ODDS OF BEING POSITIVE

S&P 500 Returns from 1926 - 2018

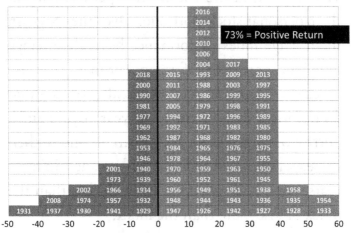

Assumes reinvestment of dividends. The S&P is unmanaged and does not incur fees.
Past performance is no guarantee of future results.

If a casino was promoting a special event where for every four bets you placed you would win, on average, three of them and that the three winning bets would payout, on average, one-third more than the one losing bet, would you be tempted to participate? While we do not recommend gambling (the odds are against you), the question above illustrates the long-term opportunity the stock market presents. It is important to emphasize that past performance does not guarantee or even predict future results. Future stock market performance may deviate from past norms.

Individual investors use the performance of indexes to measure the relative performance of their personal stock portfolio. Over the long-run the average index performance beats the average individual portfolio performance primarily because indexes are unmanaged theoretical portfolios that do not incur fees. In any given year, if your stock portfolio outperforms a comparable index then you experienced exceptional performance. In most years, your stock portfolio will gain less than the index or lose more than the index.

PROFESSIONALLY MANAGED INVESTMENTS

In today's world economy, the stock market has become increasingly volatile. Both minor and major events that occur thousands of miles away impact domestic investment markets in a matter of seconds. Because individual investors are not the first traders to respond to these events, their portfolio performance can suffer. More importantly, because individual investors are subject to emotional investing, particularly during periods of high market volatility, most individual investors' portfolios underperform portfolios managed professionally.

In 2018, DALBAR, the well-respected financial services market research firm, released their annual "Quantitative Analysis of Investment Behavior" report (QAIB). The report studied the impact of market volatility on individual investors who were managing their own investments in the stock market. According to the study, volatility not only caused investors to make decisions based on their emotions, but those decisions also harmed their investments and prevented them from realizing potential gains. In 2017, the 20-year annualized S&P return was 7.20% while the 20-year annualized return for the average equity fund investor was only 5.29%, a gap of -1.91% annualized. The bottom line is you should entrust your investment decisions to a Registered Investment Advisor who can make analytical, rather than emotional, decisions about your investments and who will always place your interests first and will not be tempted to initiate trades to generate commission.

The difference between using a Registered Investment Advisor to manage your investment portfolio and managing it yourself is a lot like the difference between using a doctor to care for a serious injury or caring for it yourself. If you had a broken arm, you would not set it yourself; you would no doubt seek out an orthopedic doctor to ensure that your arm is treated properly so it can heal correctly. Put simply, there are certain issues that are so complex and crucial that they require a specialist. There was certainly a time when people did their own investing, a time when the investment markets were less complex and volatile. During that time, it wasn't always necessary to utilize an expert to manage your investments. Today, however, trying to manage your own investment portfolio is a lot like trying to fix your own broken arm, it is not advisable. Plus, research proves professionally managed investment portfolios outperform investment portfolios managed by individuals.

When choosing a Registered Investment Advisor, require the following:

- **Contact.** You should have access to your advisor whenever you need it. If you have a question, you should be able to call, have your call answered, and get the answers you need.

- **Choice.** You should be offered multiple options and platforms, along with analysis of each option's performance and risk characteristics. There should never be pressure to settle for one option.
- **Commissions vs. Fee.** A broker charges commissions and may be motivated to serve their own interest above the clients' interest. A Registered Investment Advisor charges a fee and is therefore motivated to grow the clients' portfolio and must, by law, place the clients' interest first.

TAKING A CLOSER LOOK AT YOUR PORTFOLIO

We will analyze your entire investment portfolio as part of our planning process. Chances are you have accumulated a variety of investments over the decades and these investments are not integrated into a plan for retirement. You probably have checking and savings accounts and possibly bank CDs, a 401(k), 403(b) or TSP account, IRA and/or Roth IRA accounts, self-directed brokerage accounts, and possibly other investments. We will analyze your entire investment portfolio to determine the following: 1) portfolio risk; 2) portfolio performance; 3) portfolio suitability; 4) portfolio alternatives that may produce superior performance that contain less risk; 5) and, if your portfolio is properly aligned with a retirement plan to ensure you will never outlive your income.

CHAPTER 5 RECAP

- In today's volatile global investment markets, individuals that manage their own investments cannot react as quickly as professional investment managers and often fall victim to emotions that cause them to make poor investment decisions.
- Investment portfolios professionally managed generally outperform investment portfolios that are self-managed.
- You should be able to directly contact your professional money manager, choose from a selection of professionally managed accounts and even tailor those accounts based on your particular situation and goals.

6

REAL ESTATE: ALTERNATIVE INVESTMENTS

Jeremiah 29:5 NIV
*Build houses and settle down; plant
gardens and eat what they produce.*

Though actively managed real estate can be very
profitable, we will not cover this investment
class. Instead we will limit our discussion to two
areas: a passive real estate investment called a
Real Estate Investment Trust or "REIT" and an
investment that provides a way for individual
investors to invest alongside some of the nation's
largest institutional investors.

The long-term performance of an investment
portfolio increases and the risk decreases when

real estate is added as a component of the portfolio (see the graph below)[1].

Annualized Return (as of 12/31/17)	Standard Deviation
10.32%	9.97%

Annualized Return (as of 12/31/17)	Standard Deviation
10.46%	9.45%

Annualized Return (as of 12/31/17)	Standard Deviation
10.60%	8.97%

REAL ESTATE INVESTMENT TRUSTS (REITs)

REITs are companies that pool the capital of many investors to acquire real estate assets. This allows individual investors to invest in diversified real estate portfolios managed by professionals. REITs are required to pay distributions to investors of at least 90 percent of the taxable income each year, and are not generally subject to corporate income tax. And most importantly,

REITs are typically a non-correlated asset class, meaning assets held inside of a REIT are usually not related to the investments you own in your portfolio. Holding non-correlated assets in your investment portfolio leads to diversification, which leads to less risk over time. By adding REITs to your investment portfolio, you may lower the overall risk of your portfolio.

Why else consider Real Estate Investment Trusts? Investing in REITs has long been a strategy for providing consistent portfolio return. Because REITs typically pay stable income during good times and bad, they serve to balance the performance of the rest of your investment portfolio. But remember, like stocks, bonds and mutual funds, not all REITs are created equal. The wisest portfolio decisions are made by investors that are guided by Registered Investment Advisors - investment professionals who are committed solely to their clients' best interests.

Although there are many different types of REITs, Rhett and Mark have chosen to personally invest in the healthcare sector for two primary reasons. First, the aging of the baby boomer generation will support this sector for the next twenty-five years. This support will help offset real estate's natural tendency to fluctuate in value over time. Second, Congress will be spending an increasingly larger amount of our tax dollars on healthcare. Any vote that reduces healthcare spending is considered a vote against the American family. After defense and Social Security, healthcare has become the untouchable third rail of politics. Because of the demographics and the government-sponsored spending, we believe the healthcare sector is very nearly immune to inflation and recession and will experience growing revenues and consistent profits for decades to come.

A typical non-traded REIT may last three to eight years with limited liquidity, which is one of the downsides to this type of account. However, there are some real estate funds that allow for access to your money on a quarterly basis. In many cases Investment Strategies utilizes these types of funds to eliminate the downside of limited liquidity of non-traded REITS. These funds offer individual investors actively-managed portfolios of private real estate funds and public real estate securities selected by some of the largest and most respected institutional investment managers. These interval funds combine public and private real estate offerings and seek to optimize returns while minimizing risks. Another benefit of investing in real estate is its diversification potential. Real estate has a low, and in some cases, negative, correlation with other major asset classes. This means the addition of real estate to a portfolio of diversified assets can lower portfolio volatility and provide a higher return per unit of risk.[2]

CHAPTER 6 RECAP

- By investing in Real Estate Investment Trusts (REITs) it is possible to increase your portfolio return while reducing your portfolio risk.

- Healthcare REITs are particularly attractive given the favorable factors supporting this sector.

- An actively-managed real estate portfolio can add diversity to your portfolio and provide the benefits of income-producing commercial real estate.

[1] - *Morningstar Direct as of 1/1/1978 – 12/31/2017. Stocks are represented by the S&P 500 index. Bonds are represented by the Bloomberg Barclays U.S. Aggregate Index. Real Estate is represented by a 70% allocation in the NCREIF Property Index and a 30% allocation to the FTSE NAREIT U.S. All Equity REIT Index.*

[2] - *https://www.investopedia.com/articles/mortgages-real-estate/11/key-reasons-invest-real-estate.asp*

ANNUITIES

Proverbs 16:31 NIV
*Gray hair is a crown of splendor; it is
attained in the way of righteousness.*

Here is a hypothetical example of how a fixed-indexed annuity might help:

> *Jack and Sally are planning for their
> retirement in four years when they
> turn 66. They have worked their
> entire life and been blessed with a
> moderate retirement nest egg. While
> working, their monthly income is
> $5,000 which covers their expenses
> with a little left over each month.
> They want to maintain their standard*

of living in retirement and still have $5,000 a month of income. Their combined Social Security benefits will be $3,100 and Sally will receive a pension from her work of $1,150. But with those combined, that only adds up to $4,250/month which will leave a deficit of $750/month. This is their Income Gap. They will need to fill this gap with income from their other investments. After talking with their financial professional and looking at options, they choose to move $125,000 from Jack's 401k to a fixed-indexed annuity and start monthly, lifetime income in four years to help fill their Income Gap.

Annuities can sometimes be an item of confusion and mistrust for investors. We believe that much of this confusion comes from the fact that most investors spend the first half of their lives exposed to only stock market-based investments through their IRAs and 401(k)s, and have never had any explanation about the pros and cons of annuities. At Retirement Income Strategies we believe that annuities are just another tool in the toolbox that serve a very important role in the retirement planning process. There are a few broad types of annuities, some of which we utilize both for ourselves and our clients and some that we never recommend. In this chapter we will take a broad look at the different types of annuities and discuss both their advantages and disadvantages as well as the reasons that you might use them in your own planning.

Annuities have a bad reputation. One well-known advisor says "I Hate Annuities." But as with most things in your Retirement Income Plan, your situation is unique and a 'one-size-fits-all' approach cannot be used. A blanket statement like the one above doesn't take into account all the different parts of your situation. We agree that not everyone needs an annuity. But sometimes an annuity might be the exact thing you need.

As you progress through your working years and approach retirement, your general risk tolerance changes. When you are young, and retirement seems far away, you often utilize investments that fluctuate in value and are not necessarily concerned with volatility. Part of the reason is because when account balances are smaller you don't experience the pain of a loss as much as when account balances are larger. Another reason is because if you have many years until retirement you might feel confident that your portfolio has time to recover from losses. However, as you approach retirement, growth is still important but protecting your hard-earned money against loss becomes an increasing concern.

At Retirement Income Strategies we use fixed-indexed annuities to serve two vital roles:

1. Safe Accumulation of Assets
2. Guaranteed Income for Life

Let's begin by covering the basics of an annuity.

According to Vanguard.com an annuity is a financial product typically used by investors to save tax-deferred for retirement or to generate regular retirement income payments, helping to replace a paycheck in retirement.

An annuity is a contract between an insurance company and you. In general, you are going to give them some money (a premium) in either a lump sum or periodic payments and the insurance company guarantees you payments for the rest of your life, where you can't outlive the income. There are also options for joint-life income which are payments that will continue for the remainder of your spouse's life as well. This income stream can provide for peace of mind because of the steady, reliable income.

DEFERRED VS. IMMEDIATE ANNUITIES

A deferred annuity is when you deposit a lump sum and let it grow tax deferred until a future time to start lifetime payments. Deferred annuities can typically be started in as few as 12 months or might be deferred for many years in anticipation of a future retirement. In our retirement planning process, we will often fund deferred annuities a few years before a client retires knowing that the annuity will be used to create a monthly income stream at their chosen retirement date. Later in this chapter we will discuss how Income Riders can be used to calculate a near exact future income amount.

An immediate annuity is when you deposit a single, lump sum and begin payments soon after your initial investment. Some retirees do not have the flexibility with their retirement savings accounts to plan to purchase a deferred annuity in advance. Others might face an unexpected early retirement due to circumstances beyond their control and need income immediately. In these situations, an immediate annuity might be used rather than a deferred annuity.

Annuity Types: Variable, Fixed, and Fixed-Indexed

VARIABLE ANNUITIES

Variable annuity premiums are invested in subaccounts that are in the stock market. Typically, your contract value and income payments depend on the performance of those underlying investments. When the stock market is doing well, your contract value and income payment can go up. But the opposite is also true, when the stock market is not doing well your contract value and income payments can go down. As their name suggests, they vary with the stock market.

To be clear, we do not sell any variable annuities. Because of their volatility and their abnormally higher fees, we don't believe variable annuities serve our clients' best interests. Variable annuities do make a lot of money for the insurance company and the agent selling them, but as financial planners, we want to know what the investment is going to provide and not have to guess or hope that it provides.

FIXED ANNUITIES

Fixed annuities are contracts issued by insurance companies to people looking for guaranteed rates of return and principal protection. Often times fixed annuities are referred to as MYGAs (Multi-Year Guaranteed Annuities). They are called this because the insurance company will offer a guaranteed rate of return for a certain number of years. An investor could choose a MYGA with a term of 3 to 10 years depending on their needs. Typically, the longer the term, the higher the guaranteed interest payments are.

There are several important considerations with fixed annuities/MYGAs.

1. Interest payments are guaranteed by the issuing insurance company. It is always

advisable to choose a company with strong financial ratings.

2. Liquidity will be limited during the life of the fixed annuity. Some contracts might offer penalty-free withdrawals, while others might only allow for the interest payments to be liquid. Each contract has different terms and penalties for liquidating early.

3. Interest earned will be tax-deferred. Meaning taxes on the interest are not due until the owner receives those funds. Tax-deferral will help the account balance grow.

4. Typically, fixed annuities and MYGAs have zero management fees.

FIXED-INDEXED ANNUITIES (FIA)

A fixed-indexed annuity is a tax-deferred, long-term savings option that provides principal protection from stock market losses and growth from stock market gains. This principal protection and potential growth are two of the main reasons we utilize them in our planning process. They allow investors to completely protect their assets from downturns in the market, while still allowing for growth in years where the market gains in value.

Insurance companies that issue fixed-indexed annuities invest the majority of the premiums received into the company's general fund. The insurance company's general fund is built of a balanced and diversified portfolio of long-term bonds. A portion of the premium is also allocated to option contracts on external indexes like the S&P 500 or Dow Jones. If the external indexes rise in value, then the option contracts are exercised, and the policy holder gets to participate in some of the gains. If however the indexes drop in value the option contracts expire and the insurance company guarantees the client not to have a loss. When investing in a fixed-indexed annuity none of your money is ever invested in the stock market, that is why your account is protected from losses.

Important Considerations of Fixed-Indexed Annuities(FIAs):

1. Interest payments are guaranteed by the issuing insurance company. It is always advisable to choose a company with strong financial ratings.

2. Interest earned in FIAs is tax-deferred.

3. With a FIA, your annuity will never have a negative return, regardless of market performance.

4. FIAs typically offer 10% penalty-free withdrawals each year after the first contract anniversary. Fees apply during the surrender charge period (typically 10 years).

5. Many FIAs offer a bonus when first contributing money to the annuity.

6. Most FIAs have 0-1.1% annual fees depending on riders chosen.

As we mentioned earlier in this chapter, the annuities we do offer are Fixed-Indexed Annuities. They are investment tools that look and feel a bit like Social Security or a pension, meaning that they are designed to generate lifetime income. Every year you allow the annuity to defer, the income payments 'rolls up' by a specific amount (Income Account Rate). Let's say you have saved $100,000 and need it to generate income to meet your needs above and beyond your Social Security benefit and other investments. You give the $100,000 to an insurance company, who in turn invests it to generate growth. They usually select investments that have modest returns over long-term horizons. They use the money from the insurance products they sell to invest; use a portion of the returns to generate profits for themselves; and return a portion to clients in the form of payouts, claims, and structured income options.

INCOME RIDERS

To generate income from the annuity, you typically select something called an Income Rider. An Income Rider is a feature of most fixed-indexed annuities. Essentially, it is the amount of money from which the insurance company will pay you an income while you have your money in their annuity.

An Income Rider is typically set at the time the annuity is purchased and is usually guaranteed for a specific period of time while you are deferring the contract. For example, a 6% Income Rider would guarantee that each year you defer the annuity payments the amount of income they will pay you increases by 6%. We often compare Income Riders to the way Social Security works. With Social Security, you can begin drawing income at age 62. However, each year you wait to draw your Social Security, your benefit amount increases by 6.25% until Full Retirement Age. This is similar to the way Income Riders work. You can begin receiving lifetime income payments typically after the first 12 months of the annuity contract. The Income Rider guarantees that each year you defer the payments, your future income will be increased by a set percentage.

Remember, insurance companies make long-term investments that provide them with predictable flows of money. They like to stabilize the amount of money that goes in and out of their doors instead of paying large unpredictable chunks at once. When you opt for an Income Rider, an insurance company can reliably predict how much money they will pay you over a set period of time. It's predictable, and they like that.

In order to encourage investors to leave their money in their annuity contracts, insurance companies create surrender periods that protect their investments. If you remove your money from the annuity contract during the surrender period, you will pay a penalty and will not be able to receive your entire investment amount back. In Oklahoma, a typical surrender period is ten years.

If after three years you decide you want your $100,000 back, the insurance company has that money tied up in bonds and other investments with the understanding that they will have it for another seven years. Because they take a hit on removing the money from their investments prematurely, you will have to pay a surrender charge that makes up for their loss. During the surrender period, an annuity is not a demand deposit account like a savings or checking account. The longer an insurance company can hold your money, the easier it is for them to guarantee a predictable return on it. Depending on the company and annuity you choose, you can choose to start your lifetime income before the ten years and not pay a surrender charge.

If you leave your money in the annuity contract, you can get a reliable monthly income no matter what happens in the stock market. For many people, this is an attractive trade-off that can provide a creative solution for filling their income gap. Some people need income today, others need it in five or ten years. Everyone's situation is different and everyone's needs are different. The right annuity can help you with your income needs, whether it is filling an income gap now or providing income in the future. Rhett and Mark can help you understand and choose if an annuity needs to be a part of your portfolio.

CHAPTER 7 RECAP

- It is important to find ways to leverage your assets to meet your needs for lifetime income in retirement.
- A fixed-indexed annuity is an income-producing asset that does not subject your income to market risk, and still has the opportunity to grow.
- Be sure you understand the features, benefits, costs and fees associated with any annuity product before you invest.

BALANCING LIQUIDITY, SAFETY AND GROWTH

Ecclesiastes 3:1 NASB
There is an appointed time for everything.

June is a recently retired widow in her late sixties living by herself. She was introduced to me(Mark) through attending a Retirement Seminar. As we worked on her Retirement Income Plan, June shared with me that she routinely kept between $300,000 and $400,000 in her checking and savings accounts. She explained that if she ever needed money she knew she could get to it and that it was safe because she deposited the funds among *several different local banks. I was stunned by this piece of information.*

June explained that she received a small pension and Social Security benefits and after expenses there was a deficit of a few hundred dollars each month. What she was telling me was that safety and sufficient liquidity were the top priorities for her investments. I told her that there were investments that provided outstanding safety, more than enough liquidity for her present and possible future needs and that would provide far more return than what the bank was paying.

After several more conversations, June decided to reposition most of the bank deposits in two protected investments that I recommended. I structured monthly payments to be made from these investments into June's bank account which helped cover her extra expenses.

Liquidity, safety, and *growth* are the three defining benefits of an investment. Every investment has one or two of these benefits, but rarely all three. When we first meet with clients, we introduce this concept by looking at the Investment Triangle. (Figure 8.1)

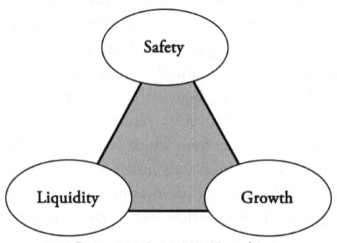

Figure 8.1 – Investment Triangle

A proper portfolio is diversified between the three sides of the Investment Triangle. For example, checking accounts, money market savings accounts and short-term certificates of deposit (CDs) are safe and liquid, but provide very low growth. On the other hand, publicly-traded stocks, bonds, mutual funds and exchange-traded funds are very liquid and can earn a high rate of return, but they are not considered safe. Third, fixed, fixed-indexed annuities and insurance products are protected by insurance companies and offer some growth but are not considered liquid. Each investor's particular goals and needs determine which investment benefits are most important. But generally, as investors age, safety becomes more important and either liquidity or growth must be sacrificed to some degree.

Understanding liquidity can help you break the risk (safety) versus return trade-off. By identifying assets from which you don't require liquidity, you can place yourself in a position to profit from relatively safe investments that provide a potentially higher than average rate of return.

Choosing safety and growth over liquidity can have a significant impact on the accumulation of your assets. If you remember the story at the beginning of this chapter, choosing liquidity was natural but costly.

The sooner you want your money back, the less you can leverage it for safety or growth. If you have the option of putting your money in a long-term investment, you will be sacrificing some liquidity, but potentially gaining both safety and growth. Rethinking your approach to money in this way can generate income while allowing the value of your asset to grow over time. The question is, how much liquidity do you *really* need?

If you haven't sat down and created an income plan for your retirement, your perceived need for liquidity is a guess. If you *have* determined your income gap and have made a plan for filling this gap, ***then you can have sufficient liquidity and still enjoy both safety and growth from your assets.***

CHAPTER 8 RECAP

- Discuss the Investment Triangle with Rhett or Mark and the concepts of liquidity, safety and growth when choosing each investment. Your customized Retirement Income Plan will help you determine how much liquidity you need so you can then take advantage of safety and growth.

PREPARING FOR THE SURVIVING SPOUSE

Psalm 55:22 NIV
Cast your cares on the LORD and he will sustain you; he will never let the righteous be shaken.

A conservative retirement plan is going to factor in one unpleasant but crucial reality - death. In almost every marriage, one spouse predeceases the other. For planning purposes, Retirement Income Strategies and Investment Strategies typically assumes husbands predecease wives for two primary reasons. First, wives usually outlive husbands of similar age by about five years. Second, wives tend to earn less over their lifetimes than their husbands and wives, therefore, stand to lose more by the death of their husbands than if the reverse occurs. However, if the wife is more than five years older than her husband or if there are extenuating circumstances that suggest a husband will likely outlive his wife then the Retirement Income Plan will assume either the husband dies the same year as his wife or the husband outlives his wife. Otherwise, it is conservative and appropriate to assume husbands predecease their wives.

Another important but unpleasant question to ask when preparing for the death of a spouse is, "what would happen if a spouse were to pass away at various crucial points in retirement?" Dependable income sources may decline or even stop when a spouse passes way. As a result, we recommend you evaluate the most-likely-case and worst-case scenarios of your income plan to be sure the surviving spouse will be able to maintain their standard of living for the remainder of their life, regardless of when their spouse passes on.

Creating plan scenarios that protect you and your spouse when the first spouse passes is a vital part of retirement planning. This is an unpleasant but critical process, and once done, will provide financial peace of mind. Rhett and Mark will evaluate and discuss with both spouses various financial outcomes should a spouse pass at different stages of life. Multiple plan scenarios can be designed to address various outcomes, ensuring that both spouses can enjoy financial peace of mind no matter which spouse passes first or when they pass.

Pre-paying for funeral and burial costs is recommended and can be done in a number of ways. The most common method to pre-pay for funeral and burial costs is to make arrangements directly with the funeral home you wish to use. If you choose this method, be sure the amounts paid can be transferred to other funeral homes if your circumstances change or if you simply change your mind about how or where you wish to be buried. If you choose this method, also be sure to use a reputable, well-established funeral home. If the funeral home goes out of business, your prepaid arrangements could go with it. Another method to pre-pay for funeral and burial costs and the one we prefer, is to purchase a final expense and burial policy. The policy death benefit can be assigned to any funeral home and all unused policy proceeds are returned to the heirs or estate. This is the most flexible and safest approach to pre-paying for final expenses. We can assist you in selecting and purchasing final expense insurance.

CHAPTER 9 RECAP

- Work with Retirement Income Strategies and Investment Strategies to understand what will happen to your income when you or your spouse pass away first.
- Some assets stop paying income when a spouse passes away; having a plan to replace that lost income is critical.
- For most situations, it is best to pre-pay funeral and burial expenses. Retirement Income Strategies recommends purchasing a final expenses insurance policy rather than working directly with a funeral home to pre-pay funeral and burial expenses.

PLANNING FOR LONG-TERM CARE COSTS

Proverbs 27:12 NLT
The prudent see danger and take refuge, but the simple keep going and pay the penalty.

One of the initial reasons that I(Rhett) became a financial advisor was because of a care need in my own family. When I was 21 years old my father had a series of health events that eventually led to him being unable to work and having an extended stay in a care facility. I remember very well not only the emotional stress that this caused, but also the tremendous financial burden that was placed on

> *our family. Today my goal is to make sure every family I meet with has a plan for retirement, has options for receiving care and has implemented their estate plan. Creating these plans will allow other families to feel more prepared when unexpected events in life take place.*

Unplanned long-term care costs can be financially devastating to seniors and they cause the greatest number of bankruptcies for this age group. Many people falsely believe that the costs associated with long-term care services are covered by health insurance and/or Medicare. And while some initial long-term care costs are covered, the vast majority of long-term care costs are not. Because long-term care costs are so substantial, long-term care insurance is expensive. Fortunately, there are affordable ways to plan for these costs.

LONG-TERM CARE COSTS

Long-term care costs are more than you think. The 2019 national median annual cost for a private room in a nursing home is $103,386.[1]

These costs alone are projected to increase at four percent a year over the next five years.

Beyond all that, older adults have the greater possibility of surgeries and hospital stays, according to The Cleveland Clinic Journal of Medicine: "Acute hospital care is fast becoming acute geriatric care: people aged 65 years or older are only 15 percent of the population but account for 44 percent of days of care in non-federal hospitals and 38 percent of discharges. In general, the elderly have longer hospital stays, incur greater costs, and have a higher risk of adverse outcomes than younger people."[2]

LONG-TERM CARE COVERAGE

Everyone should have some form of long-term care insurance. Multiple forms of coverage are best. Even if you have abundant assets to pay for your own care out of pocket, long-term care costs can become so expensive that they may eventually decimate a large estate and eliminate any hope of leaving a financial legacy. Traditional long-term care insurance, however, may not be the best answer for a number of reasons. First, the initial, affordable long-term care policy premium can morph into prohibitively expensive premiums. Second, if you have poor health or have waited too long to apply for coverage, premiums can be too high for your budget or you may be uninsurable altogether. Third, if you never use the policy all premiums paid are lost, unless you have a return of premium rider, which is very expensive.

Fortunately, other options exist to provide for long-term care costs. One of these options is a rider that can be added to a variety of fixed-indexed annuities. The annuity riders are "add-ons" that provide the policy owner and/or their spouse with the means to pay for costs like home health care, assisted living and nursing home facilities. Because these annuity riders do not require medical underwriting and are affordable they provide a good alternative for those who can no longer medically qualify for traditional long-term care insurance or those who cannot afford long-term coverage.

Most of these riders have the same trigger to begin long-term care benefits as most traditional long-term care policies. If the annuity owner, or in some cases the annuity owner's spouse, cannot perform two or more of the qualifying Activities of Daily Living (ADLs) without substantial assistance, then the amount of income the annuity generates will increase for a period of time. The Activities of Daily Living typically include bathing, dressing, transferring, toileting, continence, and eating. There are a wide variety of rider benefits, restrictions, requirements and fees, depending on the particular annuity being used. Retirement Income Strategies can help you identify the rider that will work best for your needs.

Another option that exists to provide for long-term care costs is life insurance that allows the policy death benefit to be used in advance for long-term care costs. Most older policies do not allow the death benefit to be used in advance for long-term care costs so often a new policy must be purchased to provide this benefit. The good news is that the cost of life insurance has decreased over time because life expectancies have increased. Therefore, if you are healthy it may be possible to purchase a new life insurance policy that provides for long-term care costs to replace an existing policy that does not provide for long-term care costs with little to no additional premium.

Using Required Minimum Distributions (RMDs) from Individual Retirement Accounts (IRAs) is a common source of funding to purchase life insurance. There are a wide variety of rider benefits, restrictions, requirements and fees, depending on the particular life insurance being purchased.

A third available solution to pay for long-term care expenses is a 'hybrid' policy that provides a guaranteed amount of life insurance, all of which can be used for qualifying long-term care benefits. This is a policy that helps protect your assets by using the safety of whole life insurance. There are also options that will provide lifetime long-term care benefits. You qualify to start the long-term care benefits by either being unable to perform at least two of the six ADLs or requiring care as a result of a cognitive impairment (such as Alzheimer's disease). This policy can be purchased on a single life basis, or with two insureds. It is medically underwritten which means you must be in average or better health to qualify.

CHAPTER 10 RECAP

- Although long-term care insurance is expensive, the cost of long-term care is much, much greater.
- Consider optional "add-on" riders available on fixed-indexed annuities that can provide

additional income to offset long-term care costs.

- Be sure your life insurance policy(s) allows you to access your policy's death benefit while you are alive to pay for long-term care costs. If it does not, Retirement Income Strategies can help you secure the most appropriate life insurance policy that will permit the death benefit to be used for future long-term care costs.

- Consider a special annuity that provides substantial LTC coverage but also provides return of investment if the LTC feature is never used.

- A hybrid policy uses whole life insurance and allows long-term care benefits to be paid from the policy's death benefit.

[1] - *https://www.genworth.com/about-us/industry-expertise/cost-of-care.html*

[2] - *http://www.ccjm.org/content/76/Suppl_4/S16.full*

TRADITIONAL, ROTH AND STRETCH IRAS

Proverbs 21:5 NIV
*The plans of the diligent lead to profit
as surely as haste leads to poverty.*

*Presently $22,000,000,000,000
(that's 22 trillion, in case you are
wondering) is approximately the gross
national debt of the United States.
Keep that in mind while you read
about the differences in Traditional
and Roth IRAs. The national debt
will continue to increase by tens of
millions of dollars every day. With
such high debt it is likely that taxes
will increase. Therefore, investing in*

tax-deferred or tax-free accounts is important.

Traditional IRAs were introduced in the 1970's as a way for individuals to save money each year for retirement. These accounts allowed the saver to deduct their contributions from their taxes hoping that when they retired that they would be in a lower tax bracket. Although the future of US taxation is uncertain, many people fear that taxes could be higher in the future than they are today.

Roth IRAs were introduced in the late 1990's. This type of account did not allow the saver to deduct their contributions from their taxes, but as long as they follow the rules, the distributions will be TAX FREE!

Today, most of the people we meet have the majority of their retirement money in Traditional IRAs and/or 401k's and will have to pay taxes on the distributions someday. If you still have years of saving and investing then a Roth IRA may provide substantial benefits. We usually encourage our clients to educate themselves and their children on the tax benefits of the Roth and use it when possible.

TRADITIONAL IRA AND ROTH IRA BASICS

Traditional and Roth IRAs each allow you to save money for retirement in meaningful ways, but we consider the Roth IRA to be superior. Contributions into Traditional IRAs that are made with after-tax dollars are tax deductible (but deductibility does phase out as Adjusted Gross Income rises above certain levels). Unfortunately, all withdrawals from Traditional IRA accounts are taxable and at age 70½, the IRS requires distributions from these accounts. In contrast to Traditional IRAs, contributions into Roth IRAs are NOT deductible. Because contributions are funded with after-tax dollars and no upfront deduction is given, withdrawals from Roth IRA accounts are not taxed, (as long as specific holding periods are fulfilled). In addition, the IRS does not require distributions be taken from Roth IRA accounts. At Retirement Income Strategies and Investment Strategies, we call Roth IRAs the king of accounts because their principal and accumulated growth is never taxed and this tax-advantaged account can be passed to successive generations. The chart presents the important features of Traditional and Roth IRAs.

TRADITIONAL AND ROTH IRA FEATURES

	TRADITIONAL IRA	**ROTH IRA**
WHO CAN CONTRIBUTE?	You can contribute if you (or your spouse if filing jointly) have taxable compensation but not after you are age 70½.	You can contribute at any age if you (or your spouse if filing jointly) have taxable compensation and your modified adjusted gross income is below certain amounts.
ARE MY CONTRIBUTIONS DEDUCTIBLE?	You can deduct your contributions if you qualify.	Your contributions aren't deductible.

	TRADITIONAL IRA	ROTH IRA
HOW MUCH CAN I CONTRIBUTE?	The most you can contribute to all of your Traditional and Roth IRAs is the smaller of: $6,000 (for 2019), or $7,000 if you're age 50 or older by the end of the year; or Your taxable compensation for the year.	
WHAT IS THE DEADLINE TO CONTRIBUTE?	Your tax return filing deadline (not including extensions). For example, you have until April 15, 2019, to make your 2018 contributions.	
WHEN CAN I WITHDRAW MONEY PENALTY FREE?	After age 59½.	After age 59½ and a 5-year hold period.
DO I HAVE TO TAKE REQUIRED MINIMUM DISTRIBUTIONS?	You must start taking distributions by April 1 following the year in which you turn age 70½ and by December 31 of later years.	Not required if you are the original owner.

ARE MY WITHDRAWALS AND DISTRIBUTIONS TAXABLE?	Any deductible contributions and earnings you withdraw or that are distributed from your Traditional IRA are taxable. Also, if you are under age 59½ you may have to pay an additional 10 percent tax for early withdrawals unless you qualify for an exception.	No, If it's a qualified distribution (or a withdrawal that is a qualified distribution). Otherwise, part of the distribution or withdrawal may be taxable. If you are under age 59½, you may also have to pay an additional 10 percent tax for early withdrawals unless you qualify for an exception.

If you or your spouse are covered by a retirement plan at work, your eligibility for contributions to either a Traditional or Roth IRA is reduced or phased out once your Modified Adjusted Gross Income (MAGI) rises above certain limits. If you wish to know the specific limits pertaining to Traditional or Roth IRAs, reference IRS Publication 590 or simply contact Retirement Income Strategies and Investment Strategies.

DONATING TO CHARITIES USING YOUR RMD FROM TRADITIONAL IRAs

If you're 70½ or older, you can transfer your RMD to a 501(c)(3) charity. The donation counts toward your Required Minimum Distribution but doesn't increase your adjusted gross income, which can be particularly helpful if you don't itemize and can't deduct charitable contributions.

The money needs to be transferred directly from the IRA to the charity in order to be tax-free. If you withdraw it from the IRA first and then give it to the charity, you can deduct the gift as a charitable contribution (if you use itemized deductions on your tax return), but the withdrawal will be included in your Adjusted Gross Income.[1]

ROTH CONVERSIONS

Here is a hypothetical example of how a Roth conversion might work.

Bill and Kay have been blessed with both Defined Benefit Plans (pensions) and Defined Contribution Plans (401ks) when they worked. Now that they are retired one of their goals is to preserve as much of their retirement savings as possible for their two sons. Like most families the majority of their retirement accounts are pre-tax. This means starting at the age of 70 & ½ they will be forced to take Required Minimum Distributions from their accounts, even though they don't need or want the income. Because of this they decided when they retired to take advantage of Roth Conversions. Each year they choose to convert a portion of their pre-tax accounts to Roth. They may not be able to convert all of their accounts by the time they reach 70 & ½. However, the portion that they are able to convert will not be subject to the Required Minimum Distribution rules, meaning they will not have to take money from their account. Also,

*these accounts now will be able to pass
to their son's tax free!*

Retirement Income Strategies and Investment Strategies strongly recommends that everyone who owns a Traditional IRA, 401(k), 403(b), SEP IRA or Simple IRA account, explore the possibility of converting some or all of those accounts into Roth IRAs. The major advantages of converting to a Roth IRA include:

- No required minimum distributions (RMDs)
- Tax-free growth and distributions (and, if properly structured, future generations can benefit from tax-free growth and distributions)

The sole disadvantage of converting a Traditional account to a Roth account is the tax the conversion creates. Retirement Income Strategies and Investment Strategies believes this is a worthwhile sacrifice considering the inherent, substantial advantages of Roth accounts if there are funds outside the traditional account to pay the conversion tax.

TAX ADVANTAGE OF ELIMINATING THE REQUIRED MINIMUM DISTRIBUTION (RMD)

Eliminating required minimum distributions have significant tax advantages. For example, when the owner of a $500,000 Traditional IRA turns 70½ years old they must take a required minimum distribution (RMD) of approximately $18,000. This $18,000 is added to the owner's taxable income sources to determine how much of their Social Security benefit will be taxed, and what their tax bracket will be. By eliminating RMDs, the owner may lower the amount of Social Security benefits that are taxed and lower their income tax bracket.

TAX ADVANTAGE OF TAX-FREE GROWTH

By converting traditional accounts now instead of later, you can begin realizing tax-free growth immediately. You and your heirs will never pay taxes on all future growth of converted Roth IRAs. It is an enormously powerful tool. Here's a simple example to show you how powerful it can be: *Imagine that you pay to convert a Traditional*

IRA to a Roth IRA. If you pay a 25 percent tax on that conversion and the Roth IRA then doubles in value over the next 10 years, your effective tax rate on that conversion becomes 12.5 percent tax.

Remember, while you have to pay ordinary income tax on the amount converted from your Traditional IRA to a Roth IRA, once you have done so, you have tax-free retirement funds that are permitted to grow as long as you wish and there is no requirement to withdraw the account.

Options to Reduce or Eliminate the Conversion Tax

- If you make a conversion before you retire, you may end up paying higher taxes on the conversion because it is likely that you are in some of your highest earning years, placing you in the highest tax bracket of your life. It is probable that a better strategy would be to wait until after you retire, a time when you may have less taxable income, which would place you in a lower tax bracket.
- Many people opt to reduce their work hours from fulltime to part-time in the years

before they retire. If you have pursued this option, your income will likely be lower, in turn lowering your tax rate.

- The first years that you draw Social Security benefits can also be years of lower reported income, making it another good time frame in which to convert to a Roth IRA.

- One key strategy to handling a Roth IRA conversion is to ***always be able to pay the cost of the tax conversion with outside money***. Doing the conversion in the same tax year you have a significant deduction can help you offset the conversion tax. This way you aren't forced to take the money you need for taxes from the value of the IRA.

- Starting in tax year 2017, use medical expenses that are above 7.5 percent of your Adjusted Gross Income. If you have health care costs that you can list as itemized deductions, you can convert an amount of income from a Traditional IRA to a Roth IRA that is offset by the deductible amount. Essentially, deductible medical expenses negate the taxes resulting from recording the conversion.

- If you had a Net Operating Loss (NOL) but weren't able to utilize all of it on your tax return, you can carry it forward to offset the taxable income from converting your Traditional IRA to a Roth IRA.

- If you are charitably inclined, you can use the amount of your donations to reduce the amount of taxable income you have during that year. By matching the amount you convert to a Roth IRA to the amount your taxable income was reduced by charitable giving, you can essentially avoid taxation on the conversion. You may decide to double your donations to a charity in one year, giving them two years' worth of donations in order to offset the Roth IRA conversion tax on this year's tax return.

- Certain investments can create depreciation or depletion expenses. If you make an investment that creates depreciation or depletion expenses, they can be deducted and used to offset a Roth IRA conversion tax.

The above scenarios are just some of the options for offsetting conversion taxes. If you have Traditional IRAs, Retirement Income Strategies and Investment Strategies strongly recommends you develop a plan to convert to Roth IRAs. As you approach retirement you should consider your options and make choices that keep more of your money in your pocket, not the government's.

USING ROTH IRAS TO MANAGE TAXABLE INCOME

Chances are you have income subject to taxation. If you have a Roth IRA, you have the unique ability to manage your Adjusted Gross Income (AGI). Because income from Roth IRAs is tax-free and Roth accounts are exempt from RMDs, you can choose when to take tax-free income and exactly how much to take to manage your tax bracket and taxation on your Social Security benefits.

USING INHERITED ROTH IRAS TO MANAGE TAXABLE INCOME

After you make a conversion from a Traditional IRA to a Roth IRA, you can grow this tax-advantaged account until you die. It can then be passed on to your heirs. Your heirs can then use this tax-advantaged account for income at their discretion. It is important to note, however, that non-spousal beneficiaries are required to take RMDs from a Roth IRA, or choose to stretch it and draw tax-advantaged income out of it over their lifetime.

WHEN NOT TO CONVERT

Is it always better to have a Roth IRA rather than a Traditional IRA? It depends on your individual circumstances. Some people are not adversely affected by having taxable income from an IRA. Their income might be such that Traditional IRA withdrawals and RMDs do not bump their tax bracket up or impact the taxation of their Social Security benefits. Moreover, there are situations where Traditional IRAs can be useful, as the hypothetical story below highlights:

> *There are also situations where leveraging taxable income from a Traditional IRA can work to your advantage come tax time. For example,*

Ed and Suzanne dreamed of buying a sailboat when they retired. It was something they have looked forward to their entire marriage. In addition to income annuities and investments that they accumulated for retirement income, they had also put money aside for the sole purpose of purchasing their sailboat. When they purchased the boat of their dreams, they had to pay $15,000 in sales taxes. They took a $15,000 distribution from their Traditional IRA and offset this taxable withdrawal with the $15,000 sales tax deduction. In the end, they paid zero taxes on their Traditional IRA distribution.

STRETCH IRAS: GETTING THE MOST OUT OF YOUR MONEY

In 1986, the U.S. Congress passed a law that allowed for "multi-generational" distributions of IRA assets.

This type of IRA distribution election is now commonly referred to as a Stretch IRA, Decedent

IRA or Multi-Generational IRA (hereafter, we shall refer to them according to their most common name, Stretch IRA). Stretch IRAs can be used to pass Traditional IRA assets to several generations and can be used as a lifetime income tool for the original owner, his or her children, grandchildren and great-grandchildren. Stretch IRAs are an attractive option for those who wish to create an income for their loved ones rather than leaving them a lump sum. Prior to the advent of Stretch IRAs, Traditional IRA distributions to non-spousal beneficiaries were required to be taken within five years after the death of the IRA owner. Since 1986, non-spousal beneficiaries can elect to take distributions over their lifetime, and the original IRA owner can pre-structure the distribution of their Traditional IRA as an irrevocable Stretch IRA.

CHAPTER 11 RECAP

- The differences between Traditional IRAs, Roth IRAs and Stretch IRAs are substantial and the rules pertaining to these accounts are complex. Retirement Income Strategies and Investment Strategies can assess which types of accounts make the most sense (and cents) for your particular situation.

- If you have a Traditional IRA and are older than 70½, consider directing your Required Minimum Distributions(RMD) to a charity of your choice. You can avoid taxation on the RMD amount that is given directly from an IRA to the charity.

- Usually, it is not a matter of whether or not you should perform a Roth IRA conversion, but a matter of how much you should convert and when.

- Be smart about your Roth IRA conversion: a strategic method of conversion will save you significant tax dollars. Retirement Income Strategies and Investment Strategies can show you the optimal way to convert your Traditional IRA.

- A stretch IRA, Decedent IRA and Multi-Generational IRA are different names for the same type of account. This book uses Stretch IRA when referring to these types of accounts.

- Stretch IRAs are powerful and efficient legacy tools. Beneficiaries can receive an in- heritance for life and all remaining funds at the death of the beneficiary pass to their heirs.

- Creating an efficient and defined financial legacy requires expertise and planning. Retirement Income Strategies and Investment Strategies can help you tailor a financial legacy based on your particular wishes.

[1] - *https://www.kiplinger.com/article/taxes/T032-C001-S003-donate-your-rmd-tax-free-to-charity-in-2016.html#XwoSH0SGejlh DLPI.99 and https://money.usnews.com/money/retirement/iras/articles/2017-12-04/how-to-donate-your-required-minimum-distribution-to-charity*

WHY EVERYONE NEEDS AN ESTATE PLAN

Proverbs 16:9 NLT
*In their hearts humans plan their course,
but the LORD establishes their steps.*

Let's look at two of the most famous estate planning cases ever. One case went through probate the other did not.

> *Howard Hughes died in 1976; he was an only child. He died without any estate plan whatsoever. He had no will, no trust and no children. As of today, the number of claimants on the Howard Hughes estate and their beneficiaries has grown to more*

than 1,000 people, including more than 200 relatives of Mr. Hughes. So far they have collected more than $2 billion from the liquidation of his estate. The heirs include school teachers, ministers, college professors, homemakers, architects, engineers and many more, but the profession that received the largest share of Mr. Hughes' wealth was and continues to be attorneys.

On the other hand…

John Rockefeller, Sr. was the founder of Standard Oil and the wealthiest person of his era. At the time of his death, his estate was valued at $557,905,182. After his death, the taxes and estate management costs came to $17,127,988. That sounds like a lot of money, but this is the bottom line: Rockefeller's loved ones received 97 percent of his estate, for the most part avoided the probate process, and distributed the assets in *a relatively short period of time with minimum legal fees.*

These two extraordinary cases show the results of not planning for the final distribution of estate assets versus planning for the final distribution. Regardless of the size of the estate, planning for the final distribution of estate assets will involve some costs, but that cost is a fraction of the cost of doing no final planning.

Some people read "estate plan" and have visions of castles and vaults full of gems. Then they think that "estate planning" has nothing to do with them. That couldn't be further from the truth. You have worked your entire life, and you have saved. Regardless of the total amount in your accounts, if those savings can support you during retirement (and they can) and then pass on to do good things for the people you love and the organizations you care about (and they can), wouldn't you want to be sure that happened? If so, you should construct and regularly update an estate plan.

Unfortunately, estate assets are commonly transferred to heirs after the death of the estate owner through the process known as probate.

This transfer process may or may not involve a will, can take months or years to complete, often diminishes inheritances due to fees, and is open to the public. These are just some of the reasons that most individuals that understand the probate process choose to avoid it.

PASSING ESTATE ASSETS USING A REVOCABLE LIVING TRUST

The best option for passing estate assets on to heirs is often to create and properly fund a Revocable Living Trust. This type of trust is primarily used to avoid probate.

When you establish a Revocable Living Trust you are creating a legal entity. That entity owns all of the assets that are titled in the name of the trust. The grantor(s) is the person(s) giving his and/or her assets to the trust. The grantor(s) is giving up legal ownership of their assets once those assets are re-titled in the name of the trust. The trustee(s) is the person(s) or entity(s) that is appointed to control the trust. Often the grantor(s) and trustee(s) are one and the same, and the grantor can amend or dissolve the trust at their discretion. Typically once the grantor(s) passes on, the successor trustee(s) distributes trust assets according to trust instructions. The beneficiaries are the individuals, charities, churches, etc. receiving assets from the trust, usually after the grantor passes on (We've even seen pets listed as beneficiaries).

A Revocable Living Trust has a number of advantages compared to a will. They include:

- **Avoids probate.** A will distributes assets in a set way, usually based on percentages or specific amounts. A trust can do the same without the involvement of the probate court system.

- **More flexible.** Because a trust employs the oversight of a trustee, it can perform specific duties such as paying inheritances in allotments, funding IRAs or life insurance policies, or maintaining trust property.

- **Less cost.** A trust typically costs more to set up than a will. But, in most cases, this higher set-up cost is more than offset by the savings incurred by avoiding the probate process.

- **Faster distribution.** The final distribution of estate assets generally occurs faster when a trust is employed because the extended probate process inherent with a will is bypassed.

- **More privacy.** If you wish to keep distribution details private among heirs, or if you just prefer to keep your family's finances confidential, a trust generally provides more privacy than a will.

- **More practical.** As you grow older, the management of your estate and assets might become more than you want to handle. A trust allows you to put another person, even a professional, in charge, allowing you to enjoy your retirement and focus on interests such as grandchildren and travel.

- **Peace of mind.** By putting your assets in a trust, you are also guarding your beneficiaries from legal issues or contentious decisions.

PASSING ESTATE ASSETS WITHOUT THE USE OF A TRUST

A trust may not be necessary for the final distribution of assets. For example, a will may be appropriate if someone lives in an apartment, has paid-on-death (POD) designations on all bank accounts and has beneficiary designations on all investment accounts. In this example, the bank deposits and investments will pass outside of probate because paid-on-death and beneficiary designations have greater legal weight than a will and efficiently direct the distribution of the assets. However, it is imperative that the POD designations and beneficiary forms be completed correctly and be kept up-to-date.

MINIMIZE INHERITANCE TAXES

Taxes can significantly reduce an estate, as the hypothetical example below illustrates.

> *When Bill's father passed away, he discovered that he was the beneficiary of his father's $500,000 IRA. Bill, who is 47 years old, has a wife and four children. He knew that his father had intended for a portion of the IRA to go toward funding their children's college education and the rest to go to him.*

After Bill's father's estate is distributed, Bill liquidates the IRA. By doing so, his taxable income for that year puts him in a 37 percent tax bracket, immediately reducing the value of the asset to approximately $315,000. An additional 3.8 percent surtax on net investment income further diminished the funds to approximately $296,000. Liquidating the IRA in effect subjects much of Bill's regular income to the surtax, as well. At this point, Bill will be taxed at 40.8 percent.

Bill's state taxes are an additional 5 percent. By the time taxes are deducted, Bill's income from the IRA will be reduced by 45.8 percent, leaving him with approximately half of the original $500,000. While this amount will fund most, if not all, of the college education costs of his children, it wouldn't leave much for Bill and his wife, something the $500,000 could have easily done had it not been taxed at such a high rate.

This example makes clear, leaving an asset to your beneficiaries can be more complicated than it may seem. In the case of a Traditional IRA, after estate, federal and state taxes, the asset could diminish to a fraction of its original value.

At Retirement Income Strategies and Investment Strategies one of our main goals for each client is to ensure that whatever they don't spend during their lifetime passes to their heirs in the most expedient, tax-efficient manner possible, and with the least cost and threat of contestability. To accomplish all of this, a Revocable Living Trust is usually created and tax planning is employed. There are many more details related to trusts that should be discussed with our estate planning attorney.

IRREVOCABLE TRUSTS

An irrevocable trust is a less common and less flexible type of trust compared to a Revocable Living Trust. It has its own tax identification number, the trustee cannot be the grantor and it cannot be amended. This type of trust is often confused with a Revocable Living Trust and is used for asset-protection planning.

CHAPTER 12 RECAP

- Consider an estate plan as an essential part of your comprehensive retirement plan, not something that is done just for the ultra-wealthy.

- If the only estate planning you do is to create and execute a will, you are ensuring that your estate will go through probate. Generally, probate delays the final distribution of assets for months or sometimes even years after the death of the owner of the assets. It can also diminish distributable assets due to attorney fees, and because it is a public process, it invites the public to contest the will.

- Taxes can substantially reduce the value of an estate. Proper planning for the final distribution of estate assets can minimize or even eliminate the impact taxes have on an inheritance.

- For the final distribution of estate assets, an irrevocable trust is generally less suitable than a revocable living trust.

- At Retirement Income Strategies and Investment Strategies, one of our main goals is to ensure that whatever our clients don't spend during their lifetime passes to their heirs in the most expedient, tax-efficient manner possible, and with the least cost and threat of contestability. To accomplish this, a Revocable Living Trust is often created, executed, funded and amended when required.

TALKING TO YOUR FAMILY ABOUT LEGACY PLANNING

Proverbs 3:27 NLT
Do not withhold good from those to whom it is due, when it is in your power to act.

When you think about legacy, money should be one of several topics you consider. The bigger question is, *What do you want your life to mean?* Your legacy is about more than just you, too. It's also about the family who came before you and the family you will leave behind. If you want your legacy to carry on, you must do more than use a spreadsheet and a financial plan.

Legacy, however, can also be a difficult thing to address with your family. No one wants to think about a time when you won't be around, and as such, they can be reluctant to discuss legacy at all. But if you involve them in the family side of your legacy before you broach the subject of money, it can become easier to discuss all of the legacy issues you need to address. Below you will find a guide to the four legacy-planning pillars: 1) Values and life lessons; 2) Wishes to be fulfilled; 3) Personal possessions of emotional value; and 4) Financial assets and real estate. Each pillar is followed by suggested questions to help start a fruitful discussion with your family.

PILLAR 1: VALUES AND LIFE LESSONS
Ethics and moral teachings

- What values would you like to see continued throughout your family's generations?
- What important principles guide your family?
- Is there a specific lesson or teaching that you would like to impart to future generations?
- Are there contributions to society that you have made for which you would like to be remembered?

Faith and religion

- What religious traditions would you like to see continued throughout the generations?
- Do you have religious convictions that provide guidance for your life and your family's?
- Can you recall religious stories or events from your history or past generations that have had an impact on your life?
- Do you have specific religious items that you would like to see passed down to future generations?
- Do you currently make contributions to a religious institution or organization?

Family traditions and stories

- What family history would you like to see passed down through the generations?
- Are there specific traditions or ways that you currently celebrate holidays and life events?
- Do you have annual family trips, reunions, or gatherings with friends?

- Do you have favorite family stories? Are they documented?
- Write an autobiography talking about the high and low points of your life and about how those experiences shaped you. Encourage your heirs to read this biography so they may better understand you and learn from your experiences.

PILLAR 2: WISHES TO BE FULFILLED
<u>Health and well-being directives</u>

- Do you have specific wishes for medical treatment if you become seriously ill?
- Have you named a specific health care advocate who can speak on your behalf?
- Is there a family member you might confide in or want to assist you in medical matters?
- Do you have insurance or annuity rider to cover the cost associated with long-term care?
- Do you have directives for life-support measures?

Living arrangements

- How and where do you want to live as you grow older?

- Are you considering a move to be closer to family or friends?

- Is there a specific retirement or assisted living community you have considered?

- Have you designated someone who could help you with maintenance, meals, cleaning, or security at your current residence?

- Do you have a financial plan to cover the costs associated with these living arrangements?

Final wishes and directives

- What are your final wishes and directives to be followed at the time of your passing?

- Who should be the primary person responsible to ensure that these wishes are followed?

- Do you have instructions for the executor of your will and the trustee of your trust?

- Do you have specific ideas for funeral arrangements, burial, cremation, etc.?

PILLAR 3: PERSONAL POSSESSIONS OF EMOTIONAL VALUE

Belongings of emotional value

- What items of emotional value would you like to see passed on to future generations?
- Do you have collections or memorabilia that hold emotional value to you or your loved ones?
- How would you designate the distribution of these items?
- Are your family members aware of your wishes?

Pictures, journals, and family history

- Are there items that document your life and/or family's life that you would like to see passed on to future generations?
- Where do you keep your family photos - in albums or saved electronically, or other?
- Do you have any journals, diaries, scrapbooks, family history or other important documents you would like to pass on?
- How would you designate the distribution of these items?

Household items

- Are there items in your household that hold significant emotional value, though they may not have much financial value?
- Do you have toys, books, or mementos that you would like to pass on to your children or grandchildren?
- Are there other household items such as art, crafts, or furniture that evoke fond memories for you and your family?
- Have you planned for the distribution of your household items?

PILLAR 4: FINANCIAL ASSETS AND REAL ESTATE

Items of financial value

- Are there items of financial value that you would like to see passed on to future generations?
- Do you have antiques, art, china, jewelry, or other items of value?

- Have you had these items appraised recently?
- Do you have a plan for the disbursement or sale of these items?

Residence and other real estate

- What real estate assets would you like to see passed on to future generations?
- Do you have a plan for your current residence?
- Do you have a vacation home or timeshare you would like to see passed on to your heirs?
- Do you own rental property or commercial property?

Financial assets and liabilities

- How would you like to see your financial assets (savings, investment, and retirement accounts) dispersed?
- Do you have insurance policies such as life insurance or long-term care insurance?
- How will any business interests be handled?
- Have trusts been created?
- Does the successor trustee(s) understand their role?

- Do you plan on leaving any gifts to charities or other organizations?
- What are your liabilities (mortgage, loans, automatic bill payments, etc.)?

Some additional tips for family discussion

- Aim to include all four pillars of legacy in your conversation. Too often families talk about only one part of the family legacy they want to carry on.
- Begin the family legacy conversation by talking about values and life lessons. This discussion will help bring the family together about what is important to everyone.
- Have a complete conversation about everyone's legacy priorities. You may be surprised what other family members feel is most important. For example, adult children often place a much higher value on last wishes and instructions than their parents might expect.
- Try not to wait until an illness or health scare occurs to begin your legacy conversation. Emotions and sensitivities run high at these times. Look to make

legacy discussions an ongoing event on the day after Thanksgiving or another occasion when all family members are together.

- Include grandchildren in the conversation and process to develop an ongoing tradition of family legacy discussions.

- Be creative in communicating your legacy priorities. For example, you could create a video of your parents in which they talk about their life experiences and legacy. Include some of their closest friends and other family members who can talk about your parents' lives and values.

CHAPTER 13 RECAP

- Begin a legacy discussion now. If you establish a tradition of holding an annual discussion about the four legacy pillars, your family can draw closer throughout the process and your legacy will become more secure.

- Involve all generations in your legacy discussion and be creative. Have fun with this!

GET STARTED TODAY

Proverbs 1:5 NASB
A wise man will hear and increase learning, and a man of understanding will acquire wise counsel.

When you initially meet with Rhett or Mark, the first and most critical aspect of the planning process begins immediately. We ask an abundance of questions so we can learn about your past, your family, your retirement and legacy goals, your present financial and estate plans and your present and future financial resources. Once we are equipped with this confidential information, we then apply a proprietary process that we have developed over many years of working with hundreds of families. We will create your personalized Retirement Income Plan. Though the process is similar for every client, the result is unique to each client. The Retirement Income Plan is a customized blueprint for a comprehensive retirement plan. It includes income planning, estate planning and legacy planning. The end result will provide financial peace of mind for you and your family.

Step One: Our First Meeting

Our goal during this meeting is to learn about you and your family, discuss your concerns and goals, discover your current asset allocation and your desired risk tolerance. We may also review any financial documents you bring along. More important than any documents, the primary objective of this meeting is for us to get to know you and understand your vision for your retirement and your legacy. Come as you are, and we will do the rest.

This is a list of helpful items to bring to our first meeting:

- Social Security statement if you have not already filed for your benefits
- Most Recent Payroll Stub or Earnings Statements

- Statements for 401(k); 403(b); 457; Keogh; SEP Accounts
- Statements for other IRAs and Roth IRAs
- Pension Plans/Profit Sharing Plans
- Life Insurance Policies
- Statements for Annuities
- Values and Income Amounts for Real Estate (commercial and rental)
- Brokerage Account Statements for Mutual Funds, Stocks and Bonds
- If Federal Employee: Bring Leave and Earnings Statement and Thrift Savings Plans(TSP) Statement

Step Two: Second Meeting

During this meeting we will review the personalized Retirement Income Plan we have created for you based on the information gathered at the first meeting. We will answer any questions you have and make adjustments to the plan, as necessary.

Step Three: Third Meeting

During this meeting we will determine with you which parts of your personalized Retirement Income Plan to implement, if any.

Step Four: Ongoing Meetings

After we have completed the implementation of your personal plan, we recommend meeting at least annually to review your plan and make any changes necessary. We will also review your estate plan annually and make any amendments required. If there is a need to meet more frequently than once per year, we are happy to do so. The most important thing to understand as we begin our long-term relationship is that we are here for you and your family. Whether you are a long-term client, a new client or just need a second opinion on your current situation, we encourage you to call us. We look forward to getting to know you and your family and helping you achieve financial peace of mind.

About the Authors

Rhett Wood was recruited to New York Life in 2011 where he worked for two years. During this time, he received both his insurance and security licenses. Rhett graduated with a Bachelor of Science from Southern Nazarene University and became an independent advisor with Retirement Solutions. In 2017, Rhett became the president of Investment Strategies, LLC a registered investment advisory firm in Oklahoma City. Then in 2019 started his own insurance agency called Retirement Income Strategies. Rhett has a passion for helping others reach their retirement goals, because of this he conducts numerous retirement planning programs and has been featured on many local television stations and co-hosts a weekly podcast with Mark Rose. Rhett was an award recipient of the 2018 Oklahoma NextGen under 30 Award for Finance. He serves his clients in a fiduciary capacity as an Investment Advisor Representative and also as a licensed Insurance Agent. He attends Woodland Hills Baptist Church and lives in Blanchard, OK on a family ranch where he raises Scottish Highland Cattle.

Mark Rose is a native of Ardmore, OK and earned both his bachelor's and master's degrees from The University of Oklahoma. Mark serves his clients in a fiduciary capacity as an Investment Advisor Representative who holds his Series 65 Securities License, specializing in Social Security maximization and retirement planning. Prior to this, he owned his own company and was the Program Manager for Executive

Training ~ Team Quest with The University of Oklahoma. He received both his B.A. in Public Relations and his Master's of Human Relations degrees from The University of Oklahoma. Mark has a strong background in teaching and enjoys helping his clients learn about retirement planning. He has been married for 23 years, has two daughters and attends Emmaus Baptist Church in South Oklahoma City. An interesting fact about Mark is during college, he was the OU Men's Basketball mascot – Top Daug for the 1992-1993 season. He also did two years in the Semi-pros as Sgt. Slammer for the OKC Calvary basketball team from 1997-1999.

Printed in the United States
By Bookmasters